Suburban Dog Walking

"How to Start, Develop and Grow Your Own Dog Walking Business"

By Ryan Donovan

Copyright © 2017 Ryan Donovan

All rights reserved.

ISBN: 1981105328
ISBN-13: 978-1981105328

DEDICATION

This book is dedicated to my wife, Leanne. I might be the author of the book, and these days I spend more time walking dogs than she does, but Leanne has always been the heart and soul of our business. She has a natural ability with dogs that far exceeds my own. With the growth of our family, she has scaled back on the amount of energy she is puts into the business, in order to take care of our kids. But without her strength and dedication to walking dogs for so many years, as well as her partnership in daily business decision-making, there would be no book to write.

And besides being a great dog walker and a valuable business partner, she loves me every day, even on the days I don't deserve it, and is the best Mom to our two girls.

CONTENTS

Preface: It Can Be Done — 1

Chapter 1: Our Story — 5

Chapter 2: Getting Started — 11

Chapter 3: Know the Biz You Are In — 25

Chapter 4: Nuts and Bolts — 37

Chapter 5: Growth Strategies — 57

Chapter 6: Boundaries and Attitudes — 71

Chapter 7: Win Your Mistakes — 87

Chapter 8: Growing Your Team — 105

Chapter 9: Life After Growth — 119

Chapter 10: Office and Admin — 133

Chapter 11: Afterword and Documentation — 143

Suburban Dog Walking

PREFACE: IT CAN BE DONE

Presumably, you've picked this book up because you want to earn money as a dog walker. You may have small hopes of making a few bucks on the side, larger ambitions of creating a dog walking empire, or, more likely, somewhere in between those two extremes.

People in my life are routinely surprised that I am a full-time dog walker, and that dog walking is a viable way to earn a living. It does seem like an unlikely career choice for an adult. Many people consider dog walking to be similar to a lemonade stand: the thing children do to make money in the summer.

More and more, people are treating their pets much differently now than they treated them in years past. For many, dogs are a part of the family. And for most dog owners in a city or suburb, the dog lives inside, rather than outside. A dog who is primarily inside needs to go outside to "do their business". Younger dogs especially need to get out and release their energy. If they don't, they'll take it out on their bed, your shoes, the rug, or whatever else they find.

The truth is, dog walking is a viable career choice. It can be done! That's not to say it's easy, or that success comes overnight. But it's also not rocket science. Thankfully, because, I wouldn't be qualified to do rocket science!

At the same time, dog walking isn't for dummies, especially if you're running a dog walking business with hopes to grow and succeed. You need to be smart about what you're doing, and be dedicated to learning from your successes and your failures.

If you decide to launch out as a dog walker, or even if you have already done so and you're trying to get more traction and grow your business, you will have people who either tell you it's a bad idea, or who at least are less than encouraging. That doesn't mean those people are bad people. In fact, it is likely just the opposite. They likely care a lot about your welfare, and they don't see the path to success. But there is a path to success in the dog walking business, and this book is designed to help you achieve that success.

In order to really succeed as a dog walker, you need to first take one simple evaluation step. You need to ask yourself the following question: Will I enjoy working with dogs every day? Now, that's a bigger question than it might seem, at first. You might say, "Of course, I love my dogs!" But that's not the best determiner. Do you love everyone else's dogs, too? Do you mind picking up dog poop every day, several times a day? Do you mind walking dogs that aren't nearly as pleasant as your own dog? Dogs that pull or freak out every time they see a squirrel? And are you ok having your primary work interaction be with dogs, rather than people? Are you comfortable with silence? Lots of silence?

If you don't love being with dogs, don't become a dog walker. Walking dogs is hard work, and if you don't love dogs, you will likely grow tired of spending all day, every day, with them. But if you love dogs, and are willing to walk miles and miles in all sorts of weather, then maybe becoming a dog walker is a perfect career path for you! Hopefully this book can help you make it happen.

CHAPTER 1: OUR STORY

Our story begins with adoption. With rescue. My wife, Leanne, and I got married in 2007, and wanted a dog right away. But she was in school, and we lived in an apartment, so getting a dog of our own wasn't very realistic. Finally, as her graduation date approached, we decided that we would get a dog in December. But we began to scour dog rescue websites in September, which should have been our first clue that there was no way we were going to be able to wait until December. We only made it until mid-October before we brought home our first family dog. He was a four-ish year old Akita, and we named him Levi.

Since we lived in an apartment without a yard, and since Levi was a known threat to run away, we always had to take him outside on a leash. And once you're outside with a dog on a leash, you might as well just take a walk, even if it's just around the block.

Levi was a strong, healthy, happy dog, and he loved to walk. Leanne would often walk Levi for an hour or longer. One day she remarked "I love walking Levi. I wish people would pay me to walk their dogs." And with that, the seed of our future career was born. Her words stuck in my mind. I didn't know if it was realistic or not. But I thought it might be worth a shot to start a dog walking business.

We did no market research, no real planning, and had no actual experience, outside of growing up with dogs and having our own dog. Starting a dog walking business doesn't require much overhead costs, so it seemed like a fun idea to try. A year after we brought Levi home, in October of 2010, The Vancouver Dog Walkers was launched.

We got a business license, called around and found a company willing to insure our business, and built a website. Then we waited. And waited. And no one called. We tried to do some door to door work, handing out fliers, but that wasn't particularly successful, either.

Eventually, we got our first client. He was a Jack Russell Terrier, and I'd be lying if I said the house we went to didn't feel a little suspicious. I don't know what they were doing in the back rooms of that house, but we just came, walked the dog, went home, and didn't ask any questions.

We only walked the Jack Russell a few times, but eventually, we picked up a couple regular clients. Yukon needed to be walked three days a week, and Lola needed to be walked four days a week. Shortly thereafter, we picked up a few more, and a few more, and eventually, we had a legitimate hobby-business on our hands. We weren't making a fortune, but we were able to make some money on the side to cover some of life's many expenses. I was still working full-time at another job, but thankfully, I was able to make my own schedule, and I had a lot of flexibility to help with some of the dog walks.

In December of 2012, just over two years after we launched, we realized we had a problem. Leanne was a few months away from giving birth to our daughter, Mabel, and once Mabel was born, Leanne wasn't going to have nearly as much time to devote to walking dogs. And while I did have a flexible job, I couldn't just blow off all my responsibilities and walk dogs all the time.

We went on vacation to Santa Cruz, CA, and I remember sitting in some weird Tiki restaurant, where we really hashed out whether we wanted to bring on an employee to help us continue to operate and grow the business. Prior to December, I don't think we'd ever even considered the idea that someday we may have other team members helping us make it all happen, but we did a little math, and as best we could tell, we would still make money if we hired an employee. Not as much, of course, but we'd be profitable, and we would be able to continue to grow. We decided to give it a shot.

Thankfully, that first employee we hired, Erin, was awesome. She was a joy to work with, a hard worker, and excellent with our clients. We'd like to take credit for making such an amazing hire, but the truth is, we didn't really know what we were doing. We did try our best to hire someone with good character, and who seemed like she would be a good fit with us. We sure thankful that Erin turned out to be a one-of-a-kind, awesome team member, who helped set us up on a great path.

We continued to grow over the coming years, and added other staff members eventually. It required a lot of communication with our clients, because we had transitioned from just a family business to a business where there is a diversity of team members with different personalities, strengths, weaknesses, and even dog walking styles.

Today (2017), we have been in business for seven years, have a team of 11 walkers, and in the summer of 2016, I left my other job to devote all my time to The Vancouver Dog Walkers. We still aren't rich. But we are making a livable income that allows us to pay the mortgage, the electric bill, and all the other basic expenses of life. And we've been able to provide a part-time paycheck for a bunch of other individuals and families, as well.

The success we've achieved so far did not come easy. It's required a lot of hard work and patience. The success also came a little slow, because I was only able to dedicate part of my time to our growth. Since transitioning to being fully dedicated to growing and running our business, we've seen even greater growth. The truth is, we love what we do. We get to work with amazing team members, and we get paid money to walk dogs. That's pretty incredible!

CHAPTER 2: GETTING STARTED

Ok, so you're ready to be a dog walker. Now what? What does it look like to get started? Well, like I said in the preface, the first step is to really make sure you want to hang out with dogs all day, every day. And that you want the responsibility that comes with running your own business. If you don't want to do the business side of dog walking (tracking income and expenses, responding to client calls and emails, keeping a log of walks and payments for each client, etc.), you are likely better served to work for another dog walking business in your town. But if you want to make a livable income from dog walking, you'll need to be willing to be more than just a dog walker. You'll need to be a small business owner.

In the movies and on tv, you see dog walkers in New York City or Chicago walking around with a dozen dogs on a leash, all at the same time. I'm sure that works for many people, especially if you live downtown in a big city. But that kind of dog walking doesn't make sense if you're living in an area filled with neighborhoods, where people are a little more spread out. Big city dog walking is not what we do. I call our brand of dog walking "Suburban Dog Walking".

As a Suburban Dog Walkers, we don't walk twelve dogs at a time. Generally speaking, we walk one or two dogs at a time. We drive to a client's house and walk their dogs in and around their own neighborhood. Then, we hop in our car and drive to the next client, and on and on, until the day is done. Some days the walks are near one another, and other days you spend a lot of time in the car, driving from place to place.

First Steps

The very first thing we did was select a business name. While it's tempting to try to come up with the most clever business name ever, what we really wanted was to be found in a google search. We live in Vancouver, WA (a suburb of Portland, OR). We figured that if someone was going to go online in our city to find a dog walker, they'd probably type in *dog walker vancouver wa*. Rather than try to outsmart Google, we just named ourselves The Vancouver Dog Walkers. Feel free to name your business similarly. Unless you're in Vancouver. In that case, you'll have to find your own name. There are other ways to get your business found online than just a name, so come up with a name you like, and that you think you'll still like in five years. Don't feel pressure to have the most clever business name of all-time. Just something simple and clear.

We also wanted to start out on the right side of a law. After picking a business name, and we applied for a business license through the state of Washington. You should be able to find that information on your state / city website, and most of what needs to be done to apply for a business license can be done online. It also means paying taxes (booo!). No one likes paying taxes, but it's just a part of life as citizen and business owner.

We then called around to find a company who would insure us. We ended up using State Farm, and we received a rate that was quite reasonable for what seems like pretty good coverage in all the major areas we need. There are other insurance options for dog walkers from companies that specifically focus on insuring animal-care businesses, and I'm sure you can find those with a simple Google search, as well.

The last piece of the startup puzzle, for us, was to build a website. We had a bit of an advantage, in that I've got a little bit of experience building and maintaining websites. But I don't write code, and there is a ton I don't know. And yet, the tools that exist today for creating a website are incredible, even if you're not 100% literate in the field of web design. Again, you can find all sorts of great options for easily building a website by doing a simple online search.

Sell Yourself / Be Yourself

From day one, one of the most important tasks to succeed as a dog walker is to build trust with your clients and potential clients. One of the best ways to do that is to be a real person. Be a knowable person. Build your business with your face.

What I mean is that you should make sure your clients get to know you, at least a little bit. It doesn't mean you need to invite them all over for dessert (I suppose you could try it, though). It does mean you need to let them see you. When building your website, make sure to include a picture of yourself, and some info about you. You don't have to embellish that you love dogs so much that you've rescued 582 of them, or pretend like you are some kind of doggie guru. Just be you.

If you love Star Wars, mention that in a bio about yourself. Or if you love skydiving, or swimming, or eating apple pie at midnight. Just talk about yourself. Maybe leave out the really weird stuff (I know we've all got some weird stuff). But be yourself. It helps people start to feel like they can trust you, and that you are a normal, knowable, interesting and trustworthy person.

Website

Your website is important. Very important. I know I'm no marketing genius, but I'd say it's the most important piece of marketing you can do for your business. When I built our current website, I purchased the rights to use bright, vibrant, professional images of dogs. I could use pictures I took myself, but I'm not a photographer. I spent $150 on some images. I know, for sure, that $150 was well spent.

While I just mentioned that you want to make sure your clients can get to know you a bit through your website, you really want to make the website give a positive and happy feel. People should come to your website and like what they see. If you aren't comfortable trying to build the website yourself, pay for someone to do it. Having a quality website is worth the investment. Or invest in learning how to do it. Trial and error will get you a long way. A website helps you to seem legitimate to potential clients. Conversely, not having a website will make you seem like you aren't a professional.

The primary things you want your website to do is to make potential clients feel comfortable with you. Your website should clearly and repeatedly show your contact information, as well as spell out the prices for your various services, and it should contain some information yourself, to help potential clients get a little comfortable with you before they even call. But keep it all simple, too. Beautiful pictures of happy dogs will do a lot more than a million words could do. Check out our website, www.vdogwalkers.com, to see what we've done. It's not perfect, I'm sure. But it's not bad, either.

Setting Prices

One of the big questions to solve is the question of pricing. I know every part of the US (and beyond) has different standards of living. People might pay a lot more for a dog walker in New York City than they would in Albuquerque, New Mexico. Things are just more expensive in New York.

One of the best tools at your disposal for setting prices is, again, Google. Find other dog walkers in your city, or in your general area. See what they are charging. Try to get a handful of different results, and then price in accordance with what is normal in your area. When we started in 2010, there weren't many dog walkers in Vancouver, so I took a look at what people in Portland were charging. In setting your prices, you don't need to undercut the market and be the lowest cost option you can find. I suppose that is one strategy, but once you set your prices, it's tricky to raise your prices. So set your prices in line with the market. Here is what our prices looked like to start in 2010:

	1 Dog Walk	2 Dog Walk
10 Minute Dog Walk	$12	$15
30 Minute Dog Walk	$15	$20
45 Minute Dog Walk	$20	$25
60 Minute Dog Walk	$25	$30

In January 2017, we finally raised our prices, and changed our service offerings, too. But we were careful to not lose all our current clients with the price change, so we told all our clients who were with us before the price change that they would not have their prices change for at least a year. So now, as we head toward 2018, we are preparing to finally raise the prices on the clients who have been with us prior to the start of 2017, but we've already given them a whole bonus year of discounted pricing. Our new prices and service offerings are as follows:

	1 Dog Walk	2 Dog Walk
5 Minute Potty Break	$8	$8
15 Minute Dog Walk	$14	$16
30 Minute Dog Walk	$18	$22
45 Minute Dog Walk	$22	$26
60 Minute Dog Walk	$26	$30

Because we've grown to cover our whole city, we've been able to offer a quick 5 minute option at a discounted price. The goal of that service offering is to try to grab business from people who either can't afford or don't want to afford to pay for a dog walker or dog daycare, but who also don't want their dogs in a kennel, or even just indoors, all day. It's not something we could have viably offered when we were just starting out, but since we now have staff walking in all corners of our city every day, we're able to add on the discount option and still make it a profitable and worthwhile offering.

One thing to factor in to your pricing is that the walk takes longer than the listed time. What I mean is if you have a client scheduled for a 30 minute walk, that's really 50 minutes. You need to consider the time it takes to drive to the house, and then there is also time spent leashing up the dogs, unleashing the dogs, and on rainy days, you may also spend some time drying off the dogs. Even though the walk takes 30 minutes, there are always factors that require you to spend more than 30 minutes for the walk.

Managing Expectations / Pushing Past Discouragement

Once you get your business in order, have a plan, a website, prices, and whatever else you need to get started, you still have a problem. You probably don't have any clients. Even if you have a few, you certainly don't have enough to sustain you. It takes time. There are plenty of things you can do to try to drum up business (see Chapter 5), but at the end of the day, you have remarkably little control over any other person, or what they do with their money. It takes time to grow.

Growth requires patience, because it very rarely happens overnight. Instead, it happens a little bit at a time. You never know when you will receive the next phone call from someone who wants to become a new client. I don't get calls every day. We sometimes go a couple weeks without adding new clients. But then we'll have a two week stretch where we add eight new clients. I wish I could give a great explanation for the weeks when we grow and the weeks when we don't grow, but I can't. The key is to remain patiently confident. Wait expectantly for the calls to come, and be ready to answer the phone when they do.

If you are a dog walker for long enough, there will be weeks where you lose two or three big clients. Hopefully it's not any fault of yours, although mistakes do happen. But you might have one client move, a second client lose their job, and a third client have their mother-in-law move in, all in the same week. And now those three clients who were bringing in several hundred dollars a week for you are gone. It's discouraging. Really discouraging.

It's ok. You will be ok. There are more fish in the sea, and more dogs in your city. That doesn't mean you need to pretend like it isn't a step backward. It is a step backward. And it's unpleasant. But as fast as those clients left, new ones can come. And hopefully, if you managed those relationships with your lost clients well, they may come back someday. Clients who lose their jobs typically get new jobs. Clients who have dogs that die typically get new dogs. And you just never know if it's going to work out to have Mother-In-Law in the house.

The bottom line is that you've got to manage your own expectations and emotions. Not every day is a good day or a growth day. But hopefully, with diligence and hard work, you'll have a lot more good days than bad days, and you'll see growth over the long haul.

Fake It Until You Make It

On your first day as a dog walker, you aren't going to be

an expert. Learning how to manage different dogs, different clients, and the needs of both, can really be a challenge. It's ok that you don't know everything you need to know. Learn. And in the process of learning, act like you know what you're doing. This is not the same as acting like a know-it-all. It's just simply acting like you're comfortable and confident, even if you aren't entirely comfortable and confident. If you have to give yourself a pep talk before meeting a new client, or before walking a challenging dog, do it. Does it feel weird? Yep. Does it work? Well, it certainly doesn't hurt, and, at least for many people, it can be helpful to talk through the challenging situations you are expecting, so you have a plan for how to respond. You can do it. Seriously, you can.

CHAPTER 3: KNOW THE BIZ YOU ARE IN

You might be inclined to start a dog walking business because you'd rather work with dogs than people. I can identify with that feeling. Dogs are great, and people are… people. But you've got to be careful. Even if you'd rather hang out with the least enjoyable dog than spend time around most people, you still have to make sure you grow in your ability to work with people. You don't get the opportunity to be a complete hermit, if you want to succeed.

One of the things I remind myself all the time is that at the end of the day, I'm really not in the Dog Business. I am in the People Business. Yes, I walk dogs all day long, usually by myself. As an introvert who loves to spend all day by myself, walking dogs and listening to music or to the latest podcast on my headphones, I am perfectly happy spending time by myself.

But so far, in seven years of dog walking, I have yet to see a dog pull out their wallet and pay me. Every single time I've been paid, it's been another human who has made that transaction. People pay the bills. And they decide whether they are going to continue paying you, or if they are going to stop. As much as they might like to solicit advice from their dogs on how wonderful you are as a dog walker, they won't get much help in that department, either.

Because you are really in the people business, you need to make sure you are doing everything you can to cultivate the relationships with your clients. I have five basic elements that are crucial to the human element of your business. You need to Communicate, Leave No

Trace, Be Dependable, Sell, and Care.

Communicate

The number one thing you have to do to succeed in the people business is to communicate. Communicate well, communicate quickly, and communicate often. Be in touch with your clients. Talk to them in person, by email, by text message, or whatever other means seems to work. If there is a concern you notice with a dog (bloody poop, unusually lethargic, overly aggressive behavior) let the client know right away. They may already know about the issue, but they also may not. And either way, they will be thankful that you noticed and that you communicated.

If a client calls or emails you, get back to them. As soon as you can. Don't wait a few days. Take that communication seriously. Make sure they know you will respond in a timely manner. And if it ever takes you longer than 12 hours to respond to a client, apologize for the delay.

Some of your clients, particularly Senior Citizens, will be home when you come to walk their dogs. Plan to spend a few extra minutes talking with those clients, if they are at all open to that brief conversation. Yes, it costs you a little time. But the chance to build face to face customer relationships is worth gold. Clients who know you, trust you and even enjoy you are far more likely to keep using your service for a long time. Don't rush off. Spend a few minutes, ask a few questions, and don't be afraid to share some about yourself with those clients, as well. Beyond how those relationships will be positive for your business, it is a chance to make a positive difference in someone's life. Don't overlook those kinds of opportunities!

Leave No Trace

Most of your clients will not be home when you come to walk their dogs. Instead, you'll have a key, an entry code, or some other way to get access to the dog. One of your goals should be to leave their home exactly the way you found it. If you come in and turn on a light, turn it off when you leave. If the dog has wet paw prints they leave on the floor, wipe those up. If you use the bathroom, make sure to flush. Seriously, don't forget that one, that's gross! If you need to dry a dog off with a towel, fold it up when you are finished, or hang it in the specified place.

The point is, you need to leave their space as tidy, or tidier, than you found it. This might sound crazy, but your clients will extrapolate the quality of walk, the happiness of their dogs, and the degree to which you are trustworthy, based simply on how well you clean up after yourself. There may not be much logic involved in this belief, but I've seen it happen plenty of times. You have the opportunity to make yourself look good or bad, simply by how you leave your clients home after a walk. Whatever you do, don't leave a mess. Leave each client's house just how you found it, or leave it better than you found it.

Be Dependable

One of the biggest unspoken questions your clients will have is regarding your dependability. No one wants to hire a flake. Your clients want to know they can count on you to be there when you said you would be there. For plenty of your clients, you may present the only opportunity for their dog to get out of their crate, or at least out of the house, during the daytime. Or perhaps your visit means your client doesn't have to spend their entire lunchbreak driving home to let the dog out. The last thing they want to hear is that suddenly you aren't available.

This also means taking a different view of "being sick". Yes, you will still get sick. And yes, it's possible you might get so sick that you have to cancel some dog walks. For as much as you'd like to be able to fully control your body at all times, sickness happens, and you generally don't have the chance to plan for it. But if you have a cold, or even a pounding headache, and you'd really rather stay inside, eat chicken noodle soup, and binge on Netflix, you are out of luck. Grab your Kleenex and head on out, because you've got commitments to uphold.

Now, if you are so sick that you really, really should not be out walking dogs, there's not a whole lot you can do. If you are able to have a partner, or someone who you've trained as your emergency sub, that's great. But if you don't have a partner, and you are so sick that you can't walk dogs, and can't even go visit dogs to at least give them a potty break, you had better use every avenue you have (call, text, email, etc.), to make sure your clients are aware of the situation as soon as possible. And make sure to be very apologetic, too!

Ultimately, dependability comes down to a decision. Am I going to show up? Every day? Will I be someone who takes my job so seriously, that I will do everything I can to fulfill my dog walking commitments?

What if your car breaks down? This is real life. What will you do in that event? Find a car. Ask a friend to borrow a car. Keep asking friends until you find one. Ride a bike. Rent a car. Take an Uber, a Lyft, or whatever other form of transportation that exists. Yes, it might cost you money. It might mean you end up walking dogs for a whole day, and don't make any money, or even that you lose a few dollars. I know this might sound crazy, but you've got to do it. Maintaining your dependability is worth the expense, and even worth taking a loss some days.

Sell

If you're considering a career, or have already started one as a dog walker, there's a good chance you don't see yourself as a salesperson. I know I don't. For many people, sales can be uncomfortable and awkward. But if you want to succeed, some measure of salesmanship is going to be required.

The question you must ask yourself regarding selling your service, is whether you believe in your service, and believe it is worth the price you are charging. Do you believe that someone who hires you will subsequently appreciate that their dog is getting exercise while they are busy at work? Do you think you are providing a valuable service at a fair price, so your client doesn't come home to find a mess on the rug? Do you believe that providing exercise and a mid-day break for dogs is valuable to the dog and to that dog's family? Then tell people what you do, and ask them to consider using your service.

If you tell a dog owner about your dog walking service, what is the worst-case scenario? I'd say the worst-case scenario is that they think you're crazy, tell you to get lost, and you walk away feeling bad about yourself for 5 minutes, until you get over it. But that person is rare. The more likely negative scenario is that someone says "thanks, but no thanks", or "I'll consider it", or something like that. But there's also a chance that someone will say yes. Or there's a chance someone will say "I'll consider it", and actually mean it. You might just find a new client.

If you want to succeed, you have to be willing to get a little uncomfortable, by asking people to consider using your dog walking service. And hey, they just might say yes!

Care

Care. Just care. Care about the people who have hired you. Want what is best for them. Want what is best for their dogs. Be someone who takes a genuine interest in the well-being of your client and their dogs. Don't see clients as paydays. See them as people. Care for them as people.

This isn't particularly complicated. Are you willing to care about your clients more than you care about putting money in your pockets? It's counter-intuitive, but if you do this well, you'll find yourself do better, financially, than if you didn't care at all. It is not common for a person to feel like a business cares about them. When was the last time you felt like your cable / internet provider cared about you as a person? Or how about the big box chain store where you shop for your groceries, home improvement items, or clothing? Do you feel like they care about you? Probably not.

You are uniquely positioned to be a business that cares. Did you hear that your client has been sick? Send a card in the mail. Did a previous client just tell you that have to cancel service because they lost their job? Send an empathetic email. Did your client just have a baby? Give a gift. These are all small things you can do to care for the people who have hired you to walk their dog. Be a business that takes an interest in the personal well-being of your clients. It might be a short-term cost, but it will be a long-term gain, and it will really make a difference in the lives of your clients.

CHAPTER 4: NUTS AND BOLTS

The Consultation / Meet N Greet

Call it what you want: Consultation, Meet N Greet, Introduction, etc. That first time meeting a potential new client is important. It's the ol' "No second chance to make a first impression" situation. You are sitting in front of someone who is considering hiring you to walk their dog, and the way you manage the consultation will absolutely impact whether you get hired. Here are the "5 Be's" you need to give yourself the best chance to turn that potential client into an actual client.

Be #1 - Be On Time – Or Call

If you want to start off on the right foot with a new client, show up at the time when you said you would show up. Even be 2-3 minutes early. Don't show up 10 minutes early, and don't show up 10 minutes late. This is simple, but life is crazy, and there are a thousand things that will keep you from being on time. Being on time is a way to show your potential client that you respect them, and that is one way to build trust. Being late is a quick way to erode trust.

This means you need to leave your house early, know how to get where you are going or have the address pulled up on your GPS, and factor in things like traffic and whether your gas tank is full. Again, this is all simple stuff, but it makes a difference.

Even with the best intentions, you may find yourself running late some days. This doesn't mean it's ok, and try your best to be on time, but if it happens, call and apologize. Make sure to let your potential client know what time to expect you. And call as soon as you realize you're late. If you know your day is running behind, advanced notice is helpful for your clients, and keeps them from waiting around.

In truth, you can build trust by communicating about your lateness. The phone call and the apology let potential clients know you are both a normal person, and that you are considerate and care about the needs of others. Lateness is a bad strategy, so certainly don't aim for it. But a phone call goes a long way toward redeeming your mistake.

Be #2 - Be Prepared

When you show up, have your act together. You should have some paperwork to give your potential client to fill out, containing all their contact info, the description of the services they need, and more info.

Also, be sure you have reviewed as much information as you have been given about what they need. If they told you on the phone, or in an email, that they are primarily looking for 30 minute dog walks on Tuesdays, Thursdays and Fridays, you should know that when you walk in the door. Take a few minutes before you arrive at the consultation to review what they need, so you don't walk in clueless.

When I arrive at a new client, I typically have six items in hand. I have our client intake paperwork, I have a magnet with our contact info on it, I have a check in card (which is one thing we use to communicate with our clients), I have a professional looking postcard-sized flier that contains our contact info and pricing, I have an optional credit card authorization form, and I have a lock box they can have, if they want it. (Copies of all our paperwork, as well as links to download that paperwork, can be found in Chapter 11.)

Walking in the door to meet potential clients with documents in hand is both practical and helps to create the image that you aren't a rookie (even if you are a rookie!). When you have docs and handouts, you look like you know what you are doing. You seem like a professional, not some fly-by-night, irresponsible dog walker.

Be #3 - Be Appropriately Talkative and Inquisitive

When you show up for a consultation, be prepared to talk. And be prepared to listen. But most of all, be ready to read and react to the situation in front of you. Some people want to talk, get to know you, and get comfortable with you. Talk to those people. Share with them. Be friendly and open. Don't' be afraid to have a conversation. Hopefully most of it will be about the dogs you're hoping to walk, but let the conversation go where the client takes it.

On the other hand, if you find yourself talking and talking and talking, and it feels like your potential client isn't even paying attention, stop talking. What you need to do is take your cue from the potential client. You'll have consultations that go 45 minutes. And you'll have consultations that take 5 minutes. As a generality, I've found that if I am meeting with a man, the consultation is short. If I'm meeting with a woman, the consultation more likely to go a little longer. This is a generality, so it's not entirely true, but in my experience, I'd estimate that it holds true about 75% of the time. Regardless of expectations, though, walk in ready to take the conversation wherever the client wants it to go, and to take the time, however long or short, that your client wants to take.

Be #4 - Be Honest

Honesty is the best policy. Of course you know that. There may be times where you have a potential client ask you to do something you are not comfortable doing. Don't pretend it is ok. Be honest, right away. If we have a client ask us to give their dog a medical injection, we say we can't do that, because that's a service we don't offer. If we have a client who is looking for regular Sunday visits, we have to tell them we don't do regular Sunday visits.

Honesty doesn't mean you have to be unkind. If they

ask you for a service you are not able to provide, or are not comfortable providing, it's ok to say so. But you can also say it in a positive, kind, endearing way. When someone asks us to do a medical injection, we typically respond by saying "I'm sorry, injections are something we aren't able to do. We don't have proper training to do that, and want to make sure your dogs only get medical treatment from people who have the proper training." What we have just done with that answer is that we have been honest, been kind, and also shown that we care about the well-being of their dog.

It's always possible that, by being honest, you will lose potential clients. But you're better off. Never agree to something that makes you uncomfortable, and never promise a service you can't deliver.

Be #5 - Be Humble

Maybe you've been a dog walker for a while. Maybe you just know a lot about dogs and dog behavior. Or maybe you *think* you know a lot about dogs and dog behavior.

At the consultation, the person sitting across from you is almost never looking for your advice. They are looking for you to be a dog walker. So, for the most part, you will be best served to not express your opinion about what you think would be best for their dog. They didn't call you to be an advisor. They called you to be a dog walker.

Now, if a client asks you specifically about your opinion, then you are free to share your opinion. But outside of that situation, if you hope to win a client, keep your opinion to yourself.

On the other hand, there may be occasions where you walk into a consultation, and realize immediately that the situation is bad. I had a circumstance recently, where the owner had a large Boxer who was entirely out of control. He was jumping all over me, licking me like crazy, and even putting his teeth on me. I knew in about 30 seconds that I wasn't interested in walking that dog. In that instance, I was less shy about sharing what I felt were helpful opinions. I was doing that for a few reasons. First, if they do hire me, I want to establish some ground rules right away, because what was happening from the moment I entered the door was unacceptable. And the second reason I shared my opinion is that I didn't mind if they didn't hire me. It was an out of control situation. So I spoke a little more freely, knowing they may decide to not hire me, which was certainly a fine outcome in my mind. And third, I was hoping to give them some help, because more than usual, this potential client really needed help. So far, that potential client hasn't called me back, even though we had a positive interaction and I think I gave them some helpful ideas for how to manage their unruly dog. I consider that addition by subtraction.

One More Thing – Wear Clean Socks

Ok, this isn't super important, and it's not one of the five "Be's", but whenever you show up at a new house, you never know if it's a house where you can keep your shoes on, or if they will ask you to take your shoes off. Come with the assumption that your shoes are coming off, and wear clean socks. You'll feel a lot better taking you're your shoes when you reveal clean socks, rather than socks that look like they could use a few rounds in the washer with good helping of bleach.

The Walk

If you're reading this book, I doubt you need a lot of training on how to walk a dog. And even if you did, I don't know that a book would be the most helpful way to give you that training. Beyond that, there are more than a few opinions on what is best, and you don't need to conform what you think is best to whatever I say in this book. But I do think you are well-served to have an opinion and a style, and to be able to communicate that to potential clients.

I'm going to share our "style" with you. Feel free to disagree, to see things differently, to find your own way. That's great. But here is what has worked for us. We call it the Three Point Dog Walk.

Point #1 – Walk Confident

Either you are in charge on the dog walk, or one of the dogs you are walking is in charge. Be the one who is in charge. This starts simply with the way you carry yourself. Walk upright. Walk like you know what you are doing. Be confident that you know what you're doing. I'm convinced that confidence starts in the mind, and then is demonstrated by the body. So, in your mind, you have to believe you are in control, and that you are going to succeed. I know it sounds crazy, but if you tell yourself, before you start and as you go along, that you are able, that you will succeed, that you will be in control on a dog walk, you will find yourself behaving in that manner. We have unbelievable ability to control outcomings by simply deciding that we are going to succeed.

Success does look different in every situation, so you must have realistic expectations. If you're walking a dog that pulls like crazy, you can tell yourself the dog won't pull at all, until you're blue in the face, but that will have no impact on what actually happens. That isn't a realistic goal. Perhaps what is more realistic is to tell yourself that you are not going to get frustrated when the dog does pull, but will calmly, kindly and patiently correct the dog. Or you can pick out one specific situation to solve, and then focus on that one specific thing. Perhaps the dog is super reactive to other dogs. So, get a strategy in mind for helping a dog to manage that situation well before you are in the situation, and tell yourself how you are going to handle the situation when you come across another dog. The simple act of preparing to succeed will go a long way toward your own confidence, and will pay dividends on the walk.

Beyond dog walking, simply work on building your confidence in all sorts of settings. Confidence is confidence is confidence. What I mean is that, if you have confidence in normal life circumstances, you will be better equipped to have confidence in dog walking. Personal confidence transfers from one situation to another. Success in dog walking (and in meeting new clients, for that matter), requires confidence. (It's probably safe to say confidence will play a big role in life-success, in general, so building confidence is a worthwhile endeavor, even if you never end up walking dogs, or only do so for a short time.)

Point #2 – Walk the Dog (Don't Let the Dog Walk You)

Keep in mind that you are the dog walker. The dog is not the person walker. This is an important order of operations. You are the one in charge. As such, you have the right to have expectations for how the dog walks.

For me, the best walks are when a dog is walking beside me. Not out in front, with me dragging behind. Not behind, with me continually tugging on the leash. The best walks are mutually enjoyable experiences, where the dog and the walker are both moving at the same, swift pace.

Having a dog walk beside you, rather than out in front, minimizes all sorts of problems. A dog walking out at the end of it's leash is far more likely to react to other dogs, cats and squirrels that is sees. It's also in a safer position, should an off-leash dog come charging toward you. And it allows you to maintain control and keep the dog safe, in the event that there is a driver who is not paying close attention to the road and people and around them.

You'll meet some dogs who are amazing walkers on the very first day. Those are the best. It's just a happy walk time. It's the best part of the job. You walk, the dog walks, and many happy miles are covered. But you'll also meet dogs that are so-so walkers, dogs that are bad walkers, and dogs that are terrible walkers. But no dog is without hope of being a good walker. And even if dogs have poor reinforcement of good walking habits at home, you can still find some success in helping that dog to be a good walker for you. It simply requires patience, repetition, consistency, and a lot more patience.

Point #3 – Walk Swiftly

In our dog walking, our primary goal for most dogs (unless an owner has specifically instructed us otherwise), is to get the dog as much exercise as we can, in the time we have allotted. We aim to be walking at least 3 miles per hour, which is a completely reasonable pace. Plenty of the dogs we walk are in a kennel for eight hours a day, and our visit is their one chance to drain some energy. We take that responsibility seriously, trying to get them to move as far and as fast as they can, in the time we have together.

Of course, the dogs need to stop and sniff around a little, and take care of business, as well. But that should be quick and short, so that you can get back to the business of walking. We make it our ambition to stop sparingly on our walks. Instead, we try to keep moving, as much as possible, so the dogs receive the maximum amount of exercise.

We also try to control the stops. Rather than letting a dog tell us when and where to stop to sniff and pee, we tell the dog where we are going to stop, sniff, and pee. This is another aspect to helping the dog to see that they are the one being walked, not the one doing the walking.

There will be clients who specifically ask you to let their dog take their time, sniff the roses, and just lollygag through the walk. They usually don't use the word lollygag, but it's implied. In those instances, your job is simply to do what you are asked to do. As much as you may think you know what's best for the dog, it's far better to simply follow the instructions of the owner, even if it goes against your own dog walking principles. After all, you're getting paid by the owner. Listen to their desires.

The Value of Flexibility

One of the best ways to add value to the lives of your clients (and to help them continue to use your services), is to be ridiculously flexible. Or at least, be as flexible as you can muster. Your clients don't know what tomorrow will bring. It's entirely possible that they are going to wake up at 4:00 AM to the lovely sound of a 9 year old throwing up in the bathroom. All the sudden, their plan to put in a 10 hour day at the office is off, and they will be staying home to play nurse for the day. When that happens, they need flexibility.

From what I've seen, most dog walkers require 24 hour notice for cancellations, or else they charge full price for the walk. This is, on the one hand, completely reasonable. You planned your day around their request for a walk, and perhaps even said no to other walks, because you already had a full schedule. Charging for late cancellations makes sense, and I'm sure there are plenty of people who will tell you that you should charge for those cancellations.

I am not one of those people. You can charge for late cancellations, and make that money today. But there's a good chance you'll end up losing a client, because they'll get tired of paying for a service they didn't receive. And beyond that, they will not feel endeared and indebted to you. They'll feel like it's strictly a business interaction, and that you have determined that you won't be on the short end of the interaction.

On the flip side, clients who know they can cancel their requested service will stick with you, because they know you are understanding, that you care about their circumstances, and that you won't charge them for work you didn't do.

We have a very simple policy. If you cancel before we show up at your door, there is no charge. If you cancel at the door, we charge our lowest price ($8). Although uncommon, we have had a cancellation come in while we are en route to a house. Thankfully these last minute cancellations are not common, but what is common is that, every morning, I wake up to a couple emails or text messages, requesting a change in service. Sometimes those messages are from clients needing to cancel their service for the day, but other times, it is a last minute service request. Our clients know they can request service, even on the same day, and most of the time, we can make it happen. We are flexible on late cancellations, and flexible on late additions, and it's a huge benefit to our clients, which amounts to a huge benefit to us.

Now, I'd be lying if I said we've never had anyone take advantage of our cancellation policy. A couple months ago, I had someone cancel or change their service needs five times in three days. Frustrating. And in that instance, I did have to mention that, while we love to be flexible, five late service changes in three days was pushing the boundaries of what we could accommodate. They were pretty understanding, and we haven't had nearly the same problem since that time. But most of our clients respect our flexible policy, and are conscientious to not take our flexibility for granted.

Over and over, though, we are complimented by our clients, because they appreciate our flexibility. It's one thing our clients have routinely expressed that they appreciate about our service. Yes, there are days where that kind of flexibility is an inconvenience. But most days, it's no big deal, and it has allowed us to develop long-term relationships with clients.

CHAPTER 5: GROWTH STRATEGIES

By now, hopefully you're ready to get started as a dog walker. Or maybe you have already begun walking dogs, but what you really want to do is grow. As much as you enjoy the half-dozen clients you work for, you know you are capable of handling more. So, what's next? How do you grow your business and bring in new clients?

Well, like everything worth doing, it starts with hard work. For most people, most of the time, growth doesn't come easily or quickly. In fact, even when growth is happening, it is usually three steps forward and one step back. You are always one phone call or email away from a new client who is really going to help your business. And you are equally as close to one client who is going to let you know they no longer need your services, or that they are transitioning from five one-hour walks per week, to two 15 minute walks per week.

Dog walking is an up and down business. Hopefully not because you're doing a bad job, but because people's need change. People get laid off from work. Dogs die or have an injury that keeps them from needing walks. People move out of state. There are a million reasons people may stop using your service that have nothing to do with you. So how do you grow faster than you decline?

First thing is first: there is no silver bullet. There is no promise that you will always continue in an upward trajectory. As I write, our business is a little down from where it was in the Spring. I can't point to a single mistake. And we've added quite a few new clients in that time. But we've also had a handful leave under positive circumstances, and we've had some decrease the amount of walks we're doing per week. But there are some strategies we've seen be more successful, and some strategies that have been less successful.

Successful Growth Strategies

Internet Presence

Our number one tool for growing our business has been internet search engines, most notably Google. We've made a concerted effort to get our information out there in as many places as we can, so we are remarkably searchable. We have a website. And we have a Google Business listing. We're listed on Yelp, Angie's List, and we have ads we run on Craigslist. We have a listing through Thumbtack. And anywhere else where we can list our business. We want people to find us. So, we've written our name on every internet wall we can find. These are all free. The only requirement is a little time, and a willingness to make updates when things change.

Social Media Marketing

Social media isn't just important. It's essential. So far, we've chosen to focus our attention on Facebook, although I'm sure we'd be wise to use Instagram, Snapchat, Twitter, and whatever other social media options come along. On Facebook, we post Dogs of the Week, we post dog jokes, we post local dog events, we do giveaways for leashes, and more. We try to maintain and grow a social media presence. We try to post at least three things a week. More is better. And for a lot of it, we pay a little money to get it seen by more eyeballs.

Do you realize the power of a social media site like Facebook? If I want to grow my clientele in an area of my city, I can pay to make sure more people see my posts in that part of the city. If I want to make sure every 47 year old woman in my city who loves poodles and Johnny Cash sees the picture I just posted of Fifi wearing a black jacket, I can target those people. It is a powerful tool.

To make the most of social media, and particularly the aspects of social media posting where you pay money, you're always wise to target people. I could spend money to make sure a bunch of 15 year old girls see my Dog of the Week, and I'm sure plenty of them would "like" it. But none of them will pay me to come walk their dog, because they don't have any money. Instead, my most common demographic is women who are between the ages of 24-55. Why? Because that is the demographic of most of the people who have hired us. It's not because we don't want to work for someone outside that demographic. We do! We just want to make sure we focus our attention, and our money, on the people who have proven to be most likely to hire us.

Client Referral Program

About a year ago, we developed a client referral program. For a lot of years, we assumed that clients would just pass our name along, word-of-mouth style. And time after time, when we would get hired, it was by people who had not been referred by another person, but by Google. We always wondered why we weren't getting more referrals. Our clients seemed to really love us. And certainly, they knew other people who had dogs. So why were we getting so few referrals? Well, we started incentivizing our referrals, and it has made a positive impact.

For our referral program, we offer $1 off every walk, forever, if someone refers another client to us, and that referred client uses our service 5 or more times. We don't offer a discount just for getting us someone to talk to. We offer a discount for someone who gets us a client. And $1 off, forever, is a pretty good incentive. Especially if they refer four people to us, and get $4 off forever. Or 8 people. Or 12 people. We do have some parameters for limits on the referral program, but we are even open to the possibility of someday giving someone free dog walks if they refer enough people to us. At the end of the day, it's a net-positive, so although we are losing money on the referring client, we are now, overall, making more money by having a new client.

Direct Contact

Dogs are everywhere in our world. Perhaps your town has some dog parks. Or you just see people out and about, walking dogs. They might see you too, but unless you're wearing a flashing neon sign, even if you are walking a dog, they have no idea you are a dog walker. You must tell people you are a dog walker. Directly approaching people to let them know about you and the service you offer is awkward. But it works.

It doesn't work every time. Plenty of people won't hire you. But if someone has never heard of you, they will never hire you. Letting them know you exist goes a long way toward possibly getting hired. A long way.

There are plenty of people who have never even considered hiring a dog walker. They don't know they need you, or that you even exist. All they know is that they're tired of walking the dog in the dark when they get home from work, or tired of pick up poop off the rug, because their dog was inside again for 10 hours straight. You are solution they don't even know they're looking for, and they need you to let them know you exist.

Unsuccessful Growth Strategies

Sit and Wait

If you say you want to be a dog walker, but don't lift a finger to make it happen... well, you are not going to be a dog walker. As they say in Field of Dreams, "If you build it, they will come." But if you don't build it; that is to say, if you don't give yourself an online presence, don't get out and talk to people, don't get your information into the hands of dog owners, then no one is going to call you. You might luck into walking a dog for one neighbor, through a coincidental conversation. But without the hard work to create awareness of who you are and what you do, "they won't come".

Knocking on Doors

While people do need you to let them know you exist, people are increasingly less likely to hire you when you knock on their door. I know for me, you could knock on my door and tell me you're giving away gold nuggets and a lifetime supply of chocolate for anyone who signs up on your email list, and I'm still going to tell you to take a hike.

Now, I'm no sales expert, so perhaps if you're willing to be super persistent in an entire neighborhood, and you don't mind 12 people in a row telling you to get off their lawn, you might get one client from a full day of door knocking. But I doubt it. We're an online-connected society. Don't come to my door. Connect with me online, and then I'll call you, you don't need to call me.

Direct Mail

Another idea we've tried, from which we have literally seen zero results, is direct mailing. We have tried to mail generic fliers. We have tried to hand-write semi-generic cards. We have tried to hand-write cards to specific homes where we've seen a dog in a window or behind a fence. So far, we've never even had a consultation from that methodology. It's entirely possible that we are just doing it all wrong. But from our experience, it hasn't worked. And we've certainly tried it, much to the chagrin of our pocketbook (stamps ain't cheap!)

Family and Friends

Your family and friends will be excited about the dog walking business you are starting. Right up until they feel pressured to pay you to come walk their dogs. Now, it's possible that family and friends will decide to pay you to walk their dogs. But none of them want to feel pressured to be your new big client. They'd rather just be your friends and your family.

And working for friends and family is always a little dangerous, anyway. In general, in most situations, we give 25% off for friends and family. Not to gain their business, but to minimize making money off friends and family. It's just better for the relationships to keep family and business separate. The people closest can be really enticing targets. Avoid doing this, as much as you possibly can avoid it. Friends and family don't want to feel like business targets.

More Ideas

I'll be honest, I have growth strategies I haven't tried yet. Will they work? I have no idea. Probably some of these ideas will work, and some will not. We have enough business from the growth strategies listed above that I'm usually plenty busy. But here are a few other ideas you could try to drum up business for yourself.

Apartment Managers

In our town, there are a lot of apartments that allow for tenants to have dogs. But I also know apartments hate to replace carpet, trim, and anything else a dog might ruin. Getting into the good graces of an apartment manager could mean they pass your name along to new tenants, resulting in some great business. After all, if you can provide a service that reduces that number of times they have to replace carpet or do major repairs after a tenant moves out, you might really benefit their complex.

Veterinarian Clinics

Get to know your local vets, and get them on your side. They work with dogs all day, every day. They have access to so many potential clients for you. If you can find a way to build a relationship with them, there's certainly potential that may get some excellent referrals.

Public Tack Boards

All over our town, there are public tack boards, especially in retail spaces. Most of the time, these are located near the restrooms, and there is no cost to post a flier. Now, to my knowledge, I've never purchased anything from a public tack board in a retail space. But I imagine some have done that.

At the end of the day, growth isn't easy. It does involve steps forward, and steps back, and you always hope for more steps forward than backward. Growth takes time. You can certainly expedite your own growth by getting out in front of people, letting them know about your service, and inviting them to give you a try. But you also must stay patient, and not give up when it seems difficult. You never know when the next phone call is going to come in.

CHAPTER 6: BOUNDARIES AND ATTITUDES

Boundaries

Starting anything is difficult, and in order to get some traction and see results, it can be easy to think you should take every single opportunity that is presented to you. And maybe you should. But most likely, there will be opportunities that arise that you should not take. You need to determine your boundaries. You need to know what you will do, and what you won't do. At least in some areas, those boundaries can change as your life circumstances change. But in your circumstance right now, you need to think through what is reasonable and what is unreasonable.

Days and Hours

Do you want to work seven days a week? Or are there days when you're unavailable? If you stick around long enough in the business, you will have clients and potential clients want you to walk their dog seven days a week. And wow, that's mighty tempting! Those seven walks will bring in quite a bit of money. And the only catch is, you get no days off. It's entirely possible that you're in a position where you need to work every day, and perhaps you're only working three hours a day, so although you're working all seven days of a week, you're not exactly over-taxing yourself.

You will also have clients call you, who want you to come at 6:00 AM, 2:00 PM, and then a third time at

10:00 PM. Usually it is just for a weekend, here or there, and it can be some nice extra money, if you have the availability. But it also means you are up early, and working late, each day you commit to those visits. I've done that sort of routine for two weeks straight, because I said yes, and it can get really tiring, especially if it's a 15+ minute drive just to get to the house.

The truth is, you can set boundaries on your time and your days. For us, we have set a boundary that we don't do regular Sunday walks. That means if a person calls, wanting us to come walk their dog for 60 minutes, every day of the week, I say no. I tell them we would be glad to commit to those walks Monday through Saturday, but we are unfortunately unable to accommodate the Sunday walk. And I'd say it's a 50 / 50 proposition. Fifty percent of the time, the person wants someone who can cover all seven days, and so they call somebody else. And fifty percent of the time, they are ok with walks on just six days a week. It costs us money to say no to Sunday walks. But it's saving me, in the long run, from getting completely burnt out.

The same goes for those requests for early morning and late night visits. You can say no thanks. It doesn't mean you're bad, or that you have failed to serve your client. It means you're realistic about what you can do, and what you want to do. We had a client who would need us every few months, for an early morning and late night visit, starting Friday night and going through Sunday morning. It was no big deal. I always said yes, because they lived just a mile from my house. After some time, they moved about 20 minutes further away, and were hoping we would still be able to help. But that was a situation where I had to tell them no. It simply wasn't worth the time and energy to drive out and back at those inconvenient weekend hours.

Services

One of the questions we get asked from time to time, is whether we offer overnight dog sitting. Although that's a service many dog walkers offer, it is a service we have chosen to not offer. Why not? Well, the answer is simple I want to stay at my house every night, not at someone else's house. I don't blame anyone who does want to do overnight sitting on the side. It's a great way to make some extra money. But I have a wife and kids, and I'd simply rather be home with them at night.

If I were single, I would probably be more inclined to do overnight dog sitting. It's a great way to make money while sleeping. Although, you never know what the conditions will be at the house you stay.

I said yes to a dog sitting opportunity once. And only once. I thought it was a chance to win a new client. And saying yes to this dog sitting opportunity did earn us a new client, at least for a few months. But was it worth it? Not for me.

I arrived at the house as they were preparing to leave for a weekend away. I would be staying with their two lovely, but massive, pit bulls. This is probably a good time to mention that I'm allergic to dogs. Yeah, I know, that probably makes me crazy to be a dog walker. It's almost never a problem when we're outside walking. But it's a bit of a problem when I'm staying in a house with a couple dogs who will, likely, get my allergies going.

The wife showed me around their house, and explained the sleeping arrangements. The expectation was that I would be sleeping in the bed that was in the master bedroom, and the dogs would be sleeping with me in that bed, too. It wasn't until they left, and I went to sit on the bed, that I realized the mattress was in complete distress, and you sunk immediately to the box spring. On top of that, they had not bothered to provide clean sheets, but instead, just left the same sheets on the bed that they had been sleeping in, themselves. And to make matters worse, she explained before she left, that the dogs will randomly burrow into the blankets at night, which usually will wake you up.

Somehow, none of these expectations seemed unusual to this woman, but it was far afield from anything I was prepared for. I know many people sleep with their dogs. We have two dogs. A couple big Akita's. We love them. But they don't get up on the couch, and they certainly don't get up on our bed. We've been generous enough to provide them with their own beds, after all.

Suffice to say, I slept in a recliner during my overnight dog sitting experience, and let the dogs have a good time enjoying the bed all to themselves.

It was a pretty unpleasant weekend. Lots of sneezes, uncomfortable sleeping, and a couple dogs who were a little more rambunctious than what I expected. It was a reminder to me that, while I do hope to bring on new clients, overnight dog sitting probably isn't the best option for me.

Over the years, we've been asked to do a lot of unique services, and most of the time, we're glad to accommodate. It's no big deal to feed dogs. If someone wants 20 minute visits, we're more than happy to come up with a plan for 20 minute visits, even though that's not one of our listed options. We even had one client who wanted us to come for 60 minutes. Three of the minutes would involve taking her dog out to pee, but since he hated to walk, the remaining 57 minutes we were to sit on the couch, simply petting the dog. It almost felt like stealing. On a couple occasions, while I was sitting there petting the dog, she even came home. I felt sheepish, like I'd been doing something wrong, so I asked to clarify if what I was doing was what she wanted, and she confirmed that yes, indeed, I was doing exactly what she wanted me to do. Petting a dog on a couch for 57 minutes is definitely easy money.

Discounts

One thing to be prepared for is for clients to ask for discounts. Most don't ask. But some do. So, you have to decide ahead of time, whether you will give a discount, and if so, how much. If someone wants you to come 5 days a week, and they ask for a discount, would you give them one? If so, how much? How about if someone wants two visits a day, on the days they need service? If they ask for a discount, will you give that to them?

You save yourself a lot of trouble, and a lot of fumbling over your words, when you have a clear answer for the discount you can offer, or when you know for sure that you aren't able to offer any discounts. If you won't offer a discount, you have to be willing to lose that client. But you also must make sure not to undervalue your own service. Discounts are tricky, because once you give them, they're hard to take back. They become entitlements, even two years down the road.

My general rule of thumb is that, if someone needs walks 5 days a week, I can knock off $1 per walk. I don't tell them that up front, but I agree to that if they ask. Or if someone needs 6 days a week, I will typically just give them the weekend walk at the regular rate (we generally charge an extra $5 for weekend and evening walks).

Another factor in considering whether to give someone a discount is what time of day they are looking for a walk. Our "prime time" is 11:00-1:00, so I'm unlikely to say yes to a discount for walks during that time. But if someone is looking for a walk at 10:00, or at 2:00, those are great times to give discounts, because they are harder time slots for us to fill. I'd rather be working than sitting, so even if I'm working at a slightly lower rate, there is money coming in.

The bottom line is that you should know what kind of discount you can afford and are willing to give before you are ever standing in front of a potential client. That's a simple way to set a boundary, so you don't end up agreeing to a discount that is way more than you should have given.

Accommodating Late Additions

I said earlier that one of the hallmarks of our dog walking business is that we try to be as flexible as possible. And that is true. But that flexibility has boundaries. If it's a Saturday, and I have already made plans to go watch my nephew's soccer game, I won't say yes when I receive a late call asking for help. I try to nicely express how I wish I could help, but my schedule is already full. It is not that person's business to know that my nephew's soccer game is the priority on my schedule. But I've made a commitment, and I don't have to abandon all my plans to please my client. Just because my client did not plan well, and is now in the middle of an emergency (also, it's rarely actually an emergency), that doesn't mean I must then drop everything to accommodate their needs. Most clients will be very understanding, especially if you are able to accommodate late requests many other times. And the few clients who can't accept that you have other things scheduled in your life are the sort of clients who you really won't mind losing, anyway.

Holidays

How do you handle holidays? Do you want to work on holidays? Or do you want to relax on holidays? And which holidays will you observe, versus which holidays will you work? And if you work on a holiday, do you charge the regular price, or do you have a special holiday price that is a little higher? This is just another area where you are wise to plan before the holiday comes.

We have five holidays during which, as a general rule, we do not walk dogs. Our five holidays are Thanksgiving, Christmas Eve, Christmas Day, Easter, and Mother's Day. Easter and Mother's Day fall on Sundays, so we already rarely have walks requested on those days. But if one of our clients really needs us on one of those days, we let them know, well in advance, that we won't be able to help.

Other than that, we have treated every other day the same. We do walks on New Year's Day, Memorial Day, Fourth of July, Labor Day, Flag Day, Columbus Day, and all the other days that bankers take off. We have only recently made a change, so that we will be charging an extra $5 for walks on Memorial Day, Fourth of July, and Labor Day. And we've also found that all holidays tend to be light, anyway. So, we will have a handful of walks on our schedule, but nothing like our regular days.

Attitudes

Attitude isn't everything. But it sure it an important thing. Attitude will help you win, will helping you manage the days you lose, and will make sure you're on the right track for all the days ahead of you. Here are a couple attitudes you will need to really succeed in dog walking.

Servanthood

Servanthood sounds great. Until you think about it. It's easy to say, "Yeah, yeah, I want to serve my clients." It's harder to say, "I am ok with my clients treating me like a servant." To really serve your clients, you have to come to terms with them treating you more like a servant, and less like a buddy. Because, most of the time, you aren't their buddy. You have been hired to serve them, and to serve the needs of their dogs.

That means you won't always get the benefit of the doubt. You won't be treated completely fairly. Your feelings, needs, etc., won't always be considered. Hopefully you won't be treated quite like a servant by most of your clients. As mentioned earlier in this chapter, you must set boundaries. At the same time, never start to think you have the same leeway as a member of the family. You're getting paid to take care of your clients' dogs, but that doesn't mean you'll be invited to Thanksgiving dinner.

Servanthood is meeting needs and doing the dirty work. Just recently, I went to a client's house, and their dog had thrown up in his own kennel. It was a 5 minute potty break. I'm supposed to get in, get out, and I'm not getting paid very much for this short 5 minute break, so I want to keep moving down the road. But I'm also not going to put the dog back into a kennel without cleaning out the vomit. So, I find whatever materials I can to clean it out. That visit took more than 15 minutes. It wasn't quick, and it took three times as long as it should. I didn't charge any extra. But somedays, servanthood means giving more than you're paid for, to make sure you do the very best job possible.

Gratitude

On the days you start to feel discouraged, take a few minutes and make a list of reasons you have to be thankful. The list will be long. Real long. All of us, if we try, can find dozens and dozens of reasons to be thankful. If you're a dog walker, you have even more reasons. You are getting paid real money to walk dogs!

You could be sitting at a desk, working on a spreadsheet. Or you could be cleaning toilets, doing difficult math computations, or risking your life working on high powered electrical circuits. Instead, you're getting paid to walk dogs. That is incredible. That is a reason to be thankful. Thankful that, while others you know are breaking their backs on a construction job, you're getting to enjoy the company of dogs and walk for miles and miles.

But beyond that, you've got to be grateful that someone would consider you trustworthy enough to pay you to walk their dogs, have a key to their house, and help them to manage life. What an honor! There are days when the weather is bad, when every dog on your schedule is pulling you like you're in the Iditarod, and when you wish you'd never gotten out of bed. Every job has its share of things like that. But with dog walking, for as much as you have days that are less pleasant, you will also have plenty of days that are just amazing. Show gratitude.

CHAPTER 7: WIN YOUR MISTAKES

I hate making mistakes. I'm guessing you're not too fond of them, either. It's frustrating to realize you've failed. I dread the next time I get an email or phone call from a client, letting me know something didn't go right. I think it should always be perfect, and I should never make mistakes. Unfortunately, I don't have a perfect track record. I have a good track record, and I work super hard to fix or recover from mistakes, but perfection has eluded me.

You Will Make Mistakes

If you are a dog walker, or decide to become a dog walker, you will make mistakes. You'll make mistakes you could and should have avoided. You'll make mistakes you didn't realize were mistakes. You'll make mistakes that you think weren't mistakes at all. Here are some types of mistakes you might make.

Detail Mistakes

Every client has a set of details for you to handle, and as you gain more clients, you will also have more details to remember. It's easy to make detail mistakes. You'll have clients who want you to make sure their dog receives some special item after the walk. I've had clients who always wanted us to give peanut butter filled kongs, others who wanted us to leave a treat game out for their dog to do while we left, and others who've asked us to give their dog a treat, or even some food from the fridge. Even with the best of intentions, that is the sort of detail that you will remember 99 times out of 100, but every now and then, you may just miss. It happens, and for most clients, it's no big deal. Especially if it isn't a repeated mistake. It's certainly not the worst mistake you can make, and it's rare that it's a problem, but details do matter.

Like I mentioned in Chapter 3, your goal should be to Leave No Trace. Leaving a light on that was supposed to be off, failing to hang up a wet towel, or forgetting to give the dogs a small treat are examples of Detail Mistakes. Only the most finicky of clients is going to get too bent out of shape by this kind of mistake here and there, but these mistakes do have a way of eroding your client's confidence.

There are bigger Detail Mistakes you can make, which really might be bigger problems. Failing to put a dog back in the kennel, or failing to fully secure the kennel door, could result in a dog doing some real damage to a client's home. Giving a treat to a dog that wasn't supposed to receive a treat could result in a dog having an allergic reaction (this is why we only give treats to dogs if the owner provides the treats). Forgetting to lock the front door at a client's house, leaving their house vulnerable to robbery, will absolutely be a difficult Detail Mistake for your client to handle.

Scheduling Mistakes

One of the challenging aspects to dog walking is the ever-changing schedule. Whether you have a flexible scheduling policy, or even if you require 24 hour notice for changes, you will still deal with changing needs from your clients. And every time there is a change, you have the opportunity to record that change on your schedule accurately, or you have the opportunity to record that change inaccurately. You'll also get emails from clients with a month worth of walks to put on your schedule, and in that moment when you're transcribing the request from the email to the schedule, there is the possibility of making an error. There's nothing worse than making a mistake on the schedule.

The best scheduling mistakes are when you give a client an extra walk, or when you accidentally write down the walk for Tuesday, even though it was supposed to be Wednesday. If you make a scheduling mistake by giving them more service than they asked for, or service sooner than they asked for it, you still have the opportunity to do the correct service. And you can simply give them that early walk or extra walk for free. Yes, it costs a little to do that, but most of the time, it is a "no harm, no foul" kind of mistake, where you accidentally give someone more than they asked for.

It is far worse when, through some crazy circumstance, you failed to come for a walk you were supposed to do. A couple summers ago, I had a day where I had almost nothing on my schedule. I decided to take the day to build a brick fire pit in my backyard. This was a fine plan, but in the midst of my working, I forgot completely that I had almost nothing on my schedule. Which is to say I had one 10 minute potty break on my schedule. I just missed it. Those dogs didn't get let out all day. I messed up. At about 7:00 that night, I got a phone call from that owner, asking me if I had come for the 10 minute potty break that day. I hadn't come. I completely failed. It was the worst kind of scheduling mistake. It was inexcusable. I just failed.

About an hour later, I saw that client post on social media that they were looking for a new dog walker. My heart was crushed. But I knew I deserved to lose their business. I had messed up.

If you ever get a phone call about a scheduling mistake, where you failed to show up for an agreed-upon walk, it's brutally painful. You feel dumb, you feel embarrassed, and if you're at all like me, you don't get over that mistake for a few days.

Walking Mistakes

Scheduling Mistakes are, in general, worse than Detail Mistakes, and really can cost you a client. But Walking Mistakes are, usually, even worse, and if get caught making a Walking Mistake, you can really do damage to a client relationship, and even to your reputation as a dog walker.

If you've ever walked a dog who has zero leash manners, you know how frustrating that can be. Dogs that pull like crazy, that go crazy at every other dog, cat, bird or squirrel they see, or dogs that bite aggressively at the leash, can all drive a dog walker crazy. In those moments of crazy, you can let your frustration get the better of you, and physically lash out at the dog. You might think you'd never be inclined to do that, but just remember that you haven't walked every dog. There just might be a dog that pushes you to a breaking point, where you feel your frustration boiling over. In those moments, you've got to maintain your composure. You can't let yourself correct the dog too strongly. Obviously, it's unproductive, it hurts your relationship with that dog, and it's a great way to lose a client. Beyond just simply being wrong, you've got to remember that your clients don't live in a bubble. They probably know some of their neighbors, who may be watching. You never know if they have a friend driving by at that exact moment. You just never know who is watching. You've got to keep your composure, even with the most frustrating dog.

Another Walking Mistake you can make is, somehow, to let a dog get away from you. And it can happen fast. A dog sees a squirrel, and dashes toward the bushes, pulling the leash right out of your hand. Or a dog makes a sudden stop and pulls right out of their collar. I'd like to say these kinds of mistakes are 100% avoidable, but a dog can catch you off guard, and now you find yourself holding the leash with no dog attached, or no leash in your hand at all.

I had an experience where I was walking a dog down a busy, narrow road at dusk. It was a bad situation to start with, since it was poor walking and sight conditions. As we walked along the road, we came upon an alpaca farm, which was quite a surprise to me. And it was a bigger surprise to the dog I was walking, a 120 lbs. Mastiff named Blue. In an instant, she backed out of her collar at the sight of an alpaca, and took off running down the middle of this busy road. Needless to say, I was scared for the outcome. I started running down the road, waving to oncoming cars to slow down. Another motorist stopped his truck in the road and tried to help me catch Blue, but neither of us were going to catch

Blue without some luck. I had only walked Blue a few times, so I hadn't built a strong relationship with her yet.

Thankfully, Blue ran home. She didn't get hit by a car, didn't run out to some far-off land, and the story didn't turn out bad. I was able to catch her at her house, thanks to some cheese from the fridge and a noosed leash. And the relief I felt when she was home safe was incredible. It could have turned out so bad, but in the end, everything turned out ok. Phew!

If you walk dogs long enough, you'll have a dog back out of a collar or harness, or a dog somehow slip past you out of the front door. You have to stay vigilant, so that even if a dog somehow slips the equipment you are using, that they don't get away from you.

Handling Your Mistakes

I've made Details Mistakes, Scheduling Mistakes, and Walking Mistakes. I work really hard to avoid any mistakes, but with enough days and enough dogs, mistakes happen. But it is possible to turn something bad into something good. Or at least to not waste the mistake. I'm convinced you can win your mistakes. Here's how to win your mistakes.

Own It

In our contemporary society, passing blame is par for the course. Even when someone apologizes, it is normal to point out a reason, or an excuse, for why a mistake occurred. Stop it! If you make a mistake, own up to it. Take responsibility. It blows people away when you tell them, with no excuse or explanation, "I am sorry. I made a mistake. I messed up." All of us have almost no idea how to respond, because we are so conditioned to businesses and organizations not accepting blame. It's unbelievable how well people respond to an honest apology, and to a person willing to say they deserve the blame for that mistake.

Honestly, even if you have a reasonable explanation for why you made a mistake, don't take it. Just own the mistake. One of the times mistakes most commonly occur is when a client is not clear with what they want in an email. That confusion leads to a mistake, and it can be so tempting to point the blame at the confusing or unclear email. Don't do it! It doesn't help you one bit. Sure, you might feel justified. But you did nothing to make the client feel better. You did nothing to work toward keeping the client. All you did was make sure the client knows you aren't really at fault, or at least not fully at fault.

Instead, I'd advocate owning a problem 100%. If there was poor communication from the clients stand point, which in your heart you think is the cause of that mistake, it is still true that you didn't take the step to clarify what they needed. If the problem is that they made six changes to your schedule in three days, making it hard to keep up with the million changes, don't blame them. Just take the blame. You will be shocked by how big a mistake you can make while still retaining a client, when you fully take the blame for the mistake. Most people are really forgiving, and are completely taken off-guard when a business takes responsibility, rather than passing blame or minimizing the problem.

Pay For It

There are a few ways you can pay for your mistake. If you accidentally failed to close the kennel door, resulting in damage to the client's house, pay for the damages. If you can't afford to fully pay for it, take it to your insurance. That's why you have insurance. You have insurance for mistakes. Pay for your mistakes.

As I mentioned previously, I made a mistake in failing to go to a client's house to let their dogs out for a potty break, while I was busy building a fire pit. At the time of that mistake, that client owed me $75. In my apology, I forgave that $75. I gave away $75 that I was owed, for services I had already rendered. I didn't know whether that would pay off, but I needed to find a big way to express how sorry I was for the mistake I had made. I could have given them a discount, but I felt, based on the fact that they were already on the hunt for my replacement, that I had to go the extra mile in trying to win back their trust. And I'm glad to say, I weathered that storm, and we have continued to work for them three times a week, for the last two years, since we made that mistake. The mistake cost me $75, but it didn't cost me a client.

A third way you can pay for your mistake is to give freebies going forward. Make the next walk free. Or the next three walks. Or just give a discount. It simply depends on how big the offense was, and how much they seemed to accept the apology. Recently, we had a 45 minute walk on our schedule, but we accidentally only did a 30 minute walk. In the whole scheme of things, this isn't a huge mistake. But it is a mistake. Rather than charge that client for a 30 minute walk, I charged them for a 15 minute walk. So, we made a mistake, and we paid for that mistake by giving an immediate discount. The client was pleased, and we still made a little money.

Stop It

It's one thing to make a mistake. It's another thing to keep making that same mistake. You have to learn from your mistakes, and work hard to not make them twice.

Mistakes are opportunities to learn, but they aren't guarantees that you'll learn. You must take action. One simple thing you can do is to set reminder alarms on your phone. That way, even if you get busy and might be likely to forget to follow through on your commitment, you will have a reminder pop up on your phone early enough that you can stop what you're doing and go take care of that client's needs.

Another way I make sure to avoid mistakes is that I won't respond to an email from a client asking for walks until I've written those walks down on my schedule. If I respond before writing it down, I might just forget to write it down at all.

When you make a mistake, you have to work on understanding why and how that mistake happened, and do everything you can to make sure that mistake doesn't happen in the future.

Leave It

The last thing you must do regarding your mistakes is to

leave it. That is to say, you have to just let it go. I hate making mistakes so much. When I do, my natural inclination is to dwell on my imperfection. But once I've addressed the mistake and taken ownership, paid for it in whatever way I could, and worked on ways to stop that mistake from happening in the future, I have to let it go. It won't help me to dwell on my mistake. Yes, it's possible that a mistake could cost you a client. And it's also possible, depending on the client, that the mistake could result in a poor review online, or some bad social media attention. Once a mistake has been made, though, you can't control the outcome. You can only do your part to own it, pay for it and stop it.

I've found people are extremely forgiving and understanding. They're caught off guard by apologies, by freebies, and by sincerity. It's a secret weapon in business that so few businesses seem to be employing. But if you follow these four steps (Own It, Pay For It, Stop It, and Leave It) when you make a mistake, you will live to make money another day.

Live to Make Money Another Day

"Live to Make Money Another Day". That is my slogan for all mistakes. When a mistake is made, you want to do everything you can to solve the problem, and you also want to do everything you can to put yourself in a position to minimize the money lost as a result of your mistake. When I failed to let our client's dogs out for their 10 minute potty break, I gave back $75 I had earned. In just the last 10 months, that same client has paid us $928. By giving back the $75, and by apologizing sincerely and owning the mistake, rather than passing the blame, we lived to make money in the future with that same client.

Living to make money another day isn't just about mistakes, though. It also applies to when you get late cancellations. Yes, I could tell my client how annoyed I am that they just cancelled at the last minute. And I wouldn't be lying. Late cancellations can drive you nuts. But if I bite my lip and accept the cancellation happily, I'll live to make money with that client down the road. It's not all about today. It's about the next 12 months, the next 4 years, or maybe even longer.

Recently, I received a request for a visit that we couldn't accommodate. I hate to say no. I want to always say yes. But this request just wasn't possible, this time around. I let the client know we can't meet their need on this request, and I received a very gracious response to our inability to help. Rather than simply stop with their gracious response, I replied and told them that, since we couldn't meet their need, their next visit is free. Yes, that's a short-term cost. But the last thing I want them to do is take their business to someone else. I want to let them know I value them as a client. So, it will be a short-term cost, but hopefully it pays long-term dividends. It's certainly possible that they will still seek out a different service to meet their needs, but it's less likely.

It's a widely understood fact that it is far easier and cheaper to retain a client than to get a new one. Whether you find yourself managing a mistake, or just trying to make sure you retain a client, rather than losing a client, think long-term, rather than short-term, and do what you can in order to live to make money another day.

CHAPTER 8: GROWING YOUR TEAM

Everything I've written so far is foundational to the success of your dog walking business. And every part of it can be done with just one person walking dogs by themselves. You can make a nice little income as a dog walker by yourself. If you're able to average seven clients a day, who pay you an average of $20 each, that's $140 a day. Or $700 week, if you work 5 days a week. Now, if you're able to work 52 weeks a year, you will have made

$36,400. That's no fortune, but it's an income, and it will go a long way toward paying your bills. However, it's not the outer limit of your income potential.

There are three basic ways to continue to increase your income. One way is to walk more dogs. Perhaps you can walk 10 dogs per day, at an average of $20 per walk, which would give you $200 a day, $1000 a week, and $52,000 a year. But it also means, if each of those ten walks averages 30 minutes, and if you walk a normal pace of 3 miles per hour, that you will be walking 15 miles a day. Maybe *your* body can handle that many miles day after day after day, but mine can't. I can do 6, 8, or even 10 miles on any given day. I think my personal record is around 14 miles in a day. But I can't do 14 miles day after day after day. Even 10 miles, day after day, is physically challenging.

Another possible way to make more money is to charge more for your services. That works, to a point. But if there are others in your town who are also walking dogs, you have to be careful to not price yourself so high that no one can afford to hire you.

The third option is to add more people to your team. It means you make less money per walk, but it also means you have potential to continue to grow, without burning your body out. This is the route I took.

Figure things out for yourself, first. Don't get ahead of yourself.

There is a reason the idea of growing your team is toward the end of the book, rather than the beginning. Before you try to add someone to your team, you need to know what you're doing, and establish some trust with the people in your market. Before you're ready to bring on team members, you should have spent adequate time walking dogs yourself.

So, when should you bring someone on to help? My recommendation would be to not even consider it until you are at or near your own capacity. Yes, adding team members means you have help with the work, and allows you to grow. But it also means you are sharing the profit, and at the same time, increasing your risk and your responsibility. The last thing you want to do is hire someone with a promise of a certain number of hours per week, and not be able to provide those hours. Nor do you want to give away all the hours you should be working, yourself, and cease to make much money at all.

Once you have reached, or are nearing, your own personal capacity for dog walking, that's the time to hire.

Hiring Options

When you decide to hire, there are a couple options. One option, which is most common in the dog walking field, is to bring someone on as an independent contractor. That means they are technically their own dog walking company, who is contracting with you. They are responsible for paying their own taxes, managing their own clients, and basically working with you. This is one model, and it seems to be the most common, but it is not the kind of hiring I would recommend.

Instead of bringing on people as independent

contractors, another option is to hire people as employees. Depending on where you live, it likely means you have to change your business license to be able to hire employees. And there is probably a fee to do that. It also means you will be paying a portion of that employee's social security, as well as paying in to things like unemployment. It costs money to have employees.

In large part, I believe it's best to hire employees rather than bring on "independent contractors", because those "independent contractors" are generally being treated as employees, only without the benefits and protections of workers who are employees. Employees must be paid a minimum wage. Employees receive Social Security compensation from their employers. Employees are eligible for Worker's Compensation, in the event of a workplace accident. These are protections, which are due to someone being treated as an employee. If a person is working for you as an independent contractor, but they aren't free to also grow their own dog walking business, or work for other dog walking businesses, or to set and keep their own hours on their own terms, then the truth is, they are being treated like an employee, and should be given the same benefits and protections that employees receive.

I know this can be challenging. In my home state of Washington, our minimum wage will be $11.50 in 2018, $12.50 in 2019, and $13.50 in 2020. Also, starting in 2018, employees will be entitled to a small amount of paid sick leave. That all is expensive, especially because we are committed to paying our employees at least a bit above minimum wage. But just because something is expensive, doesn't mean it can't be done. It just means our profit is a little lower than we would prefer, and that we need to charge our clients a little more than we would prefer. But since we've spent so many years building a great reputation, we can charge a little more than some others who are new to the business.

Hiring employees isn't cheap, but it's the best way to grow your business and really flourish. We've grown to have a team of 11 part-time walkers, who each work between 12-30 hours a week, with most averaging right around 20 hours each week.

How to Pay

We pay our employees an hourly wage. The way it works, for us, is that when an employee arrives at the first dog on their schedule for the day, they clock in (shout out to TSheets, an awesome mobile app we use to manage our employee time sheets). Then they are on the clock as the walk dogs and travel between each dog. We don't pay mileage, but we pay our employees during their drive time.

One of the biggest challenges when we were first looking to hire our first employee was figuring out their payroll. There are taxes to set aside each paycheck. And money to be paid into Social Security. And some other things, too. In adding employees, one thing I knew I didn't want to do was learn how to properly do payroll. Instead, we hired a local payroll company. We submit hours for our employees on the 1st and 15th of the month, and they provide checks, or direct deposit, for our employees. They also take care of setting aside the proper amount for each employee, and send that money to its proper place, along with filing the correct paperwork. For all that work, it costs us just under $40 per pay period. $40 is certainly not a tiny cost, but the hours it would take me to do it all, and to make sure it's all correct, is a much bigger headache than $40. For us, that is money well-spent, so I can focus on the job of dog walking, managing dog walkers, and working with clients and potential clients.

Hire Character!

Hiring people isn't easy. You post a job, probably to some online job board (we've found Craigslist and Indeed to be affordable options, at this point), and then receive resumes. We also ask our employee prospects to answer a small handful of questions, which at least give us a chance to get a little more information about them than we can get from just a resume. But even so, there have been many times we were excited about a prospective employee, only for them to really underwhelm us at an interview. On the other hand, we've decided to interview people who we were a little less excited about, and we've ended up hiring those people.

As much as we want to hire people who have some skill in walking dogs, that isn't our number one priority. Our top priority is hiring people we trust. For one thing, all our employees have a key to our house, and are in and out of our house all the time, since our office is based out of our house. But not only do they hold a key to our house, but they also hold keys to many of our clients' houses, and more than that, they hold the power to make our business thrive or to make our business sink. A dishonest person can really create significant problems for us by acting dishonestly. So, we work hard to try to figure out if the person we're meeting with is willing to be completely honest, or if they're more likely to act dishonestly. Never hire a dishonest person.

Do Your Homework

When we're considering a potential employee, we try to do everything we can to check them out. One of the first things I do is I try to look someone up via social media.

You can sometimes learn a lot about a person by the way they present themselves publicly on social media. A person's social media account can help them get hired, or it can help us be sure we would never hire them. I remember one applicant whose Facebook profile picture was of her with a beer stowed in her shirt, while she held up two middle fingers to the camera. Now, people are welcome to present themselves however they want on social media. But that's certainly not a person who I'm prepared to hire. If nothing else, their inability to see that their picture is inappropriate is likely to manifest itself down the road in our business.

On the other hand, you can also see positive attributes about a person by scanning their social media. You can see positive interactions between people. You can perhaps see that someone is socially conscious, while also remaining respectful of other viewpoints. You can see that a person has hobbies and interests.

Beyond just Facebook-stalking potential employees, though, we ask for professional references (former teachers, employers, pastors, co-workers), and we ask those references questions about what they've seen in the life of this prospective employee. We try to uncover any flaws or concerns in the short time we have that reference on the phone.

And finally, we run a background check on all employees. In the state of Washington, we can run a background check through the Washington State Patrol, and it's currently only $10 per person. We typically explain during the interview that we will be running a background check, which allows that person to explain anything we may find. It's a pretty simple tool we use to make sure we don't end up hiring someone who has a record of doing the wrong thing. And it certainly puts our clients mind at ease to know we've taken the steps we can to make sure the people entering their homes to walk their dogs are safe, responsible and trustworthy.

Hands on Training / Re-Training

When we bring someone on our team, we don't just set them free to go walk dogs on their own. Even if we bring someone onto our team who has spent years as a dog walker, we will typically have them shadow us and our other team members for at least two weeks. For one thing, when you're meeting 20 new dogs in 5 days, it can be tough to keep them all straight. And for each dog, there is a small set of details to remember, and it takes time and repetition to remember the details.

We also want our employees to learn what it looks like to have high expectations for a dog. We want them to grow in their own confidence in managing dogs of all shapes, sizes and temperaments. Much of their learning will take place on their own, once they're set free and no longer need to shadow someone, but we hope they see from us what is possible.

Whenever an employee is meeting a new dog, we never send them to that dog without a proper introduction. It doesn't matter if they've been with us for 3 weeks or 3 years, when we are introducing a new dog to them, they go with someone who already knows that dog. Or if it is the very first walk ever with that dog, they come with me. At this point, I manage all the new dogs, and train all our employees on new dogs. This way we can make sure all the information from the consultation is fully transferred to our team members, insuring that the dogs receive the treatment their owners have asked us to give them.

Love Your Team

One of the best aspects to growing your team is the opportunity it provides to invest in the lives of the people who will be working for you. We've been remarkably blessed with some incredible employees, and we've seen them grow and develop in great ways. Each person you bring on your team has a story, and each person has goals and desires, whether they realize it or not.

Part of the role you play as an employer is to help provide a way for your team members to achieve their goals. We've had some team members come on board while they are completing their education, and we've been thrilled to watch them eventually transition off our team, into their new career path. We've had others come on board as a means to make a supplementary income for their families, to help pay the mortgage, the expenses of a child who is going to college, or to get free from debt. We love helping in that way. We've had others still who have come on board either in their retirement or near-retirement years, and they're thankful to have a supplemental income, while also having a job that helps them maintain their health.

It's incredible to be a part of caring for and helping the people on your team. One of the other unique aspects of bringing on employees is that you get great a chances to talk, and to have a positive influence in the lives of your employees. If you're introducing an employee to a new dog, and taking a 60 minute dog walk with them, a few well-timed questions can open up some significant dialogue, providing you with the chance to care for the heart-needs of you team members. It's truly a privileged position to be able to love and care for your team members, and at the same time, to be loved and cared for by your team members.

CHAPTER 9: LIFE AFTER GROWTH

The opportunity to bring on team members to help your dog walking business continue to grow is awesome. Yes, it's a challenge to do it right, but it is also amazingly rewarding and fun. Hopefully, if you do it right, you create a mutually beneficial situation for yourself and those who come onto your team.

Reality Check: Employees Can't Care As Much As You Care

You started the business. You have given every ounce of your being to make this business thrive. You've worked long, hard and sometimes unpleasant hours, and done jobs you didn't enjoy, just to build the business to the point where you can hire employees. No matter who you hire, they won't have that history. They won't have nearly the amount of blood, sweat and tears invested. It would be impossible for them to care as much as you care.

Hopefully you hire employees who care a lot. The ideal employee works super hard, doesn't complain on the hard days, and does everything they can to help the business succeed. The aim is to hire people who exhibit this kind of behavior. And yes, these people do exist.

And yet, even if you hire a tremendously hard-working and dedicated employee, the nature of being an employee, rather than an owner, is that, from day one, that employee knows they can pull the plug and walk away at any time, for a thousand reasons. So, don't be surprised when your employees care less that you think the should care. It's ok. They're normal, and you're normal. Unless they are owners, they can't possibly care about the business as much as you.

Pros and Cons

Pro #1 – Increased Profits

The whole point of bringing on employees is to increase profits. If you bring on employees and subsequently, decrease profits, something has gone horribly wrong. But unless you make a mistake of over-paying your team members or under-valuing your service, bringing on employees should help you see a bump to your bottom line.

Every time an employee is walking, as long as they are making less money than you are charging for the walk, you are making a profit. So, for example, when we charge $18 for a 30 minute walk, we assume that walk requires one of our team members to spend roughly 50 minutes, between drive time and leash up time. If the walker is paid $12.50 an hour, it costs us about $10.40 for their time. Once we factor in the cost for payroll taxes, the true cost for that employee to do a 30 minute walk is about $12. That leaves a $6 profit from that walk. On the one hand, it can be difficult to accept that you only make 1/3 of the profit you would make it you did the walk yourself. On the other hand, you made 1/3 of the profit, but didn't have to do the work!

As you continue to grow and add team members, you will make a profit on each walk from each of your team members. That's growth. That is how you create a sustainable and increasingly profitable dog walking business.

I still remember the first time I was at lunch with a friend, and realized that even while I sat and ate lunch, I was still actively making money. It was like magic! I was relaxing with a cheese burger, and at the same time, the money was still coming in.

Pro #2 – Your Employees Make Money

Yes, it is super cool to see your own profits increase, and if you don't see your profits increase, you wouldn't take on the challenge of having employees. At the same time, it's not all about you and making your pockets deeper. By bringing on employees, you are uniquely positioned to provide for their needs.

In our situation, all our employees are part-time. That means, when we are hiring, we are looking for people who are wanting a part-time, supplemental job. And there are plenty of people who are looking for that exact type of employment. Perhaps they have a spouse or significant other who is the primary bread-winner in the family, but they want to contribute. Or perhaps it is someone who is in school, and who wants a job that both allows them to further their education, and also to pay some bills. A part-time dog walking position isn't the perfect position for everyone. But it is a fantastic position for many people.

By providing part-time employment, you are helping families to pay their mortgage, to pay off debt, to set some money aside for vacation, to pay for their children to go to college, or even to grow their retirement as they prepare for life beyond work. Whatever the situation, it's incredibly fulfilling to have the chance to help provide for others by creating jobs.

Pro #3 – Employees Can Have Great Ideas and Develop Great Client Relationships

You may have a ton of great ideas for how to continue to develop and grow your business. But for all the great ideas you have now, and will have in the future, there is still tremendous value in having others on your team, who will provide ideas you would have never had. It doesn't mean every idea your team members have will be a good idea, or that you'll be able to take all the ideas. But you don't take all your own ideas, either. It simply deepens the pool for ideas, by having more people thinking and offering suggestions.

Your employees will also be able to interact with your clients in unique ways. Allowing our employees to have interaction with our clients was one of the hardest elements of control for me to give up. If I am the sole person to interact with our clients, I can control what is said, and I can do my best to make sure I don't say the wrong thing at the wrong time. If I allow my employees to have more of that communication, either through text messaging, writing notes, or even by phone call, I lose control. And yet, so far, we've had nothing but positive things come from having our employees interact with our clients.

In fact, many of our clients have really come to trust the team members they interact with regularly, even if the primary means of interaction is simply through scribbled notes. Far from hurting trust with our clients, the chance for our clients to interact with our employees has really opened up trust.

Con #1 – Employees Require Management

On the one hand, it can seem like bringing on employees just means more people to do the work. And that is true, but it doesn't mean you'll have less work. It just means some of your work will be different work. You now must manage those employees. You need to do things like track hours, do training and re-training, write their schedules, manage their days off, and make sure they are doing the job to the standard you expect.

That all takes work. Lots of work. Managing employees requires you, or someone, to always be on-call when they are working. You never know when an employee is going to have an unexpected challenge arise. And while you can empower employees to make plenty of judgment calls, you are the boss, and there will be times when your employees don't know the correct answer to the circumstance, and need someone with authority to make the final decision.

You also never know when you are going to wake up to a text message or email from an employee who came down ill in the middle of the night, and is now not able to do their job for the day. There's no one else to solve that situation. You didn't ask for the problem, nor did you do anything wrong to create the problem. But here it is, and you have to deal with it. Managing employees certainly comes with it's share of challenges.

Con #2 – Employees Aren't You

You rarely hire clones. You hire people with their own strengths, weaknesses, abilities, and inabilities. And no matter their makeup, one thing is for certain: Your employees aren't you. That is to say, they <u>all</u> will do things a little differently than you do. You can train and explain until you are blue in the face, but your employees will remain unique and distinct people, with unique and distinct skill sets and personalities.

That doesn't mean you can't do significant training. You can, and you must. You must try to impart as much knowledge and preparation into their minds as you can, so they each have the best chance to succeed. But you aren't going to succeed at fundamentally changing a person. And that's actually a good thing.

If you are able to embrace the unique qualities and the strengths that each of your team members bring to the table, you will be stronger than if you were given the opportunity to hire clones. Just because your employees don't perfectly emulate the way you do what you do, doesn't mean they aren't doing great things. It just means they do great things a little differently.

Con #3 – Employees Leave

Hiring employees in a small business is a little like bringing on new family members. In our situation, our home is our office. All our employees have a key to our house, and are in and out of our house every week. They are an everyday presence in our lives. And eventually, they all will leave.

We love the people who work for us, and so far, we've been tremendously blessed to have low turnover. We wish all our employees stayed forever, but that is simply not realistic. In our case, some have left after finishing school, others because they need to find a full-time opportunity, and still others because they are just ready to be done walking dogs in the rain (we do live in WA state, after all). In any event, it's always hard to see employees leave, because it's a little like losing a family member.

Employees Make Mistakes

Certainly, the fact that employees make mistakes could be listed as a con. It's so hard when your employees mess up. Employees make all the same kinds of mistakes you can make, which are detailed in Chapter 7. Employees can make Detail Mistakes, Schedule Mistakes, and Walking Mistakes. Every single day, when you send employees out to do work, the range of possibilities for mistakes is endless. They could accidentally do a 15 minute walk, when it was supposed to be 30 minutes. They could forget to turn off the bathroom light after using it. They could have a dog get away from them, and call you because the dog they were walking is now lost in some neighborhood. By taking on employees, you are agreeing to allow those people to make mistakes that hurt your business. And if you give them enough time, they will make mistakes. Hopefully most don't lose dogs. But having an employee means you are out of control of their decision making. You are now, to a point, along for the ride.

One of the first things I remind myself whenever an employee makes a mistake, is that I also have made and will continue to make mistakes. I've found that helps me in figuring out how to handle an employee who makes a mistake. It grows my compassion and empathy, because the fact of the matter is, I make my fair share of mistakes, too. In fact, because I have more opportunity, I probably make more mistakes than any of my employees. I am certainly not perfect.

That doesn't mean I don't take employee mistakes seriously. It is necessary to kindly confront an employee who has made a mistake, to help them see the problem and make sure it doesn't happen in the future. And it's certainly possible that an employee makes a mistake so egregious that they need to be fired or suspended. We've never had to fire an employee, but we have suspended an employee for a week. It was for a significant error in judgment, which resulted in a dog getting away and being picked up by animal control. It wasn't good. In fact, we would have been well within our rights to fire that employee. But because we felt this mistake was out of character, and we had never had a significant mistake from that person previously, we decided to give that employee a second chance. After the suspension, that person responded very well, and we've never had anything remotely close to a repeat of that mistake. (And most thankfully, the dog was returned to her owner, and the owner was remarkably gracious with us!)

When employees make mistakes, the same principles from Chapter 7 apply. Whenever one of my employees makes a mistake, that means we, as a business, messed up. I don't get to simply blame an employee. Instead, I take responsibility (own it) myself, pay for the mistake, stop it from happening again, and move on (leave it). With the example of the dog that got away from our employee, on the basis of his negligence, I went and met with that client. I apologized sincerely. Even though I wasn't the person who made the mistake, I hired the person who made the mistake. That meant it was my mistake. I paid for the mistake. In that case, the owner took her dog to the vet to get treated for injured paws. I wrote a check immediately and covered that cost, without being asked. I made sure it would never happen again, by first, suspending that employee, and transitioning our best and most tenured walker to be the primary walker for their dogs. And then I stopped worrying about it. We've maintained that client, and we continue to do $88 worth of service for them every single week.

Employees Really Are Wonderful

There are tremendous liabilities and challenges associated with bringing on employees. But even so, our business is so much better, and so much stronger, because we have a team of awesome employees. Given all the pros and cons, my absolute recommendation is to not be afraid of hiring people to help you succeed. It's so rewarding and fun, and if you are careful in who you pick to join your team, the blessing of growing your team and your profits will far exceed the challenge of managing those employees.

CHAPTER 10: OFFICE AND ADMIN

You are smart. All of us are smart. But no matter how smart you are, you are also limited. If you have one client you work for, it's possible to keep 100% of the information in your head. You can likely keep track of how much money you are owed, what days you are walking that dog, and even details like the owner's name and email address. As you grow, the ability to keep that information in your head will reduce. You just can't remember everything. For that reason, you must make sure to keep good records.

Keeping good, tidy records isn't glamorous. For a lot of people, it's not much fun at all. You probably didn't get into dog walking for the administrative side of the job. But it's of great importance! It's like eating your vegetables. It's not as delicious as a cheeseburger, but if you don't take care of the office and administrative side of the business, you'll die young.

Sorry if that sounds overly dramatic, but it's really the truth. You can be the greatest dog walker in the world, but if you don't have a record of how many walks you've done for a particular client, or how much they do or don't owe you, you are already a sinking ship. Without good record keeping, your business won't last.

Keeping Track

You need to keep track of every single walk you do for your clients. If you do a walk, there should be a record that shows you did that walk. And you should also keep track of every payment you have received from every client, too.

When we started, we used a three ring binder to track everything. Each client had a file in that binder, and we tracked their walks and payments. It started as a 1" binder, then a 2" binder, then 3" and eventually 4". And then, one day, we realized that if our house burned down, or if we somehow lost that binder, we would have no idea how much any of our clients owed us. Also, we didn't want to buy and maintain a second notebook.

As a result, we created a spreadsheet to track each client's walks and payments. There is a link to a template of that spreadsheet in the last chapter. You are welcome to download the exact spreadsheet we use to manage our clients and use it for yourself. It works like a charm!

There are quite a few apps available that will track and manage your walks, invoicing, and more. But for that convenience, those apps will charge you some of your hard-earned cash. It's amazing the tools that can be created in a program like Microsoft Excel, that allow you to hold off on paying a monthly fee to someone else!

One of the challenges of keeping good records is simply the regular routine of sitting down to do the work. At the very least, you must update all your records once a week. As you grow, you will need to keep updated records daily, or at least most days of the week. You cannot afford to get behind in your record keeping.

Keeping Track – Walks

You need to have some system for logging each and every walk you do for each of your clients. I would recommend logging the date of the walk, the length of the walk, the person who did the walk, the cost of the walk, and whether that walk has been paid for, or is pending payment. You want to have fast access to all the details, and this kind of record keeping will allow you to do that.

Keeping Track – Payments

It is vital that you keep good record of the payments you receive from each of your clients. Don't just rush to take those payments to the bank. Make sure they are written down in an organized fashion. We write down the payment, and make sure to mark the type of payment, too. We accept cash, checks, Paypal payments, and we also are able to bill a credit card directly. Whatever way you receive a payment, make sure to log that payment with as much detail as you can.

Keeping Track – Income and Expenses

Every day, you have money coming in. And plenty of days, you also have money going out. You need to buy poop bags, ink cartridges, waking shoes, and so much more. Those are business expenses. You need to track every expense, so you know exactly how much money you are making, both so that you know, and so that you can properly pay your taxes. Paying taxes is the right thing to do, but paying more tax than you should is a bad plan. It you spent $30 on advertising, that is $30 less profit you made. If you fail to track that expense, you will pay taxes on that money. If you properly account for that as an expense, you will save money on taxes.

At the end of this book, there is a link to a downloadable Income and Expense Report Spreadsheet. It's simple. Track all the money that comes in, and all the money that goes out. That will help you on tax day, and it will also give you clarity about how much money you are actually making, after you take out all the expenses from any given month.

Keeping Track – Client Information

You need to keep track of each client's information. Ideally, you will have their contact info, vet info, emergency contact info, and more. You don't just want to receive that information. You want to have access to that information.

One of the simplest ways to manage all that information is by scanning all the documents you receive from clients. In addition to that, we also maintain a document that has the addresses for all our clients. All our team members have access to that information. They are all able to see, at any time, the addresses for all our clients.

Keeping Track - Mileage

One other detail you need to track is the miles you drive. Every mile has value. The government sets the value, and you can deduct the business miles you drive for the year, again lowering your tax bill. You can track miles on paper, with a little mileage booklet, or you can use an app to track your mileage. Whatever you do, make sure to track those miles, because it will save you a ton of money on tax day!

First Non-Walking Hire

Eventually, you will need to hire people to help you do more than just dog walking. For us, we prioritized hiring administrative help. We brought on an administrative assistant, and it has been a tremendous help to have someone responsible for making sure all our details are in order, and all our walks, payments, income and expenses are tracked. Every week, our administrative assistant keeps track of the walks we have done, all the payments we've received, and much more. If I need to make a flier, I give our admin assistant the basics of what I'm looking for, and she does the job. It's been an amazing help to our business, in terms of keeping us on track.

As you grow, there will be a few "non-walking" employees that you may want to bring on board. Perhaps you'll want to hire or promote a person to help train your walkers. You may also want to hire someone to help manage the business, manage schedules, manage employees, etc. But before any of those hires, my recommendation is to bring on someone who can manage the basic, day to day administrative tasks. Administration will help your business to thrive if it is done well, and if administration is done poorly, you'll find yourself in a lot of trouble. And hiring administrative help frees you up to put your time and attention to the business development and employee training, which are far tougher to hand off!

Clocking In and Out

One challenge of having employees is to manage when they clock in and clock out. When we first brought on employees, we were managing their timesheets via text message. That plan worked when we had one employee, and even when we had three employees. But there came a time when we needed to find a more practical way for our team members to clock in and out each day. We use an app, TSheets, which is simple, and allows our team members to easily clock in and out on their phones, and makes it easy to track everyone's hours. It's pretty helpful!

Online Backup

One of the best things you can do with all your business documents and spreadsheets is to back it up online. We use Dropbox. It's amazing. I can access 100% of our business documents and spreadsheets from my phone, it is all backed up, including older versions of each document. I never have to worry that if I lose my computer, or lose a notebook, that all my business documents are gone. It's all backed up for $10 a month. Dropbox is a great option, and I'm sure there are plenty of other similar online backups that exist, too, that would be worth the small expense. I use Dropbox every single day to access our documents, and it helps me keep everything well-organized.

The Bottom Line

You must keep your records and information organized and up to date. For many, it will seem like the most boring and tedious part of the job, but you will sink or swim in direct proportion to how well you execute on your administrative organization. Good administration is vital to the success of your business.

CHAPTER 11: AFTERWORD

What a privilege it is to be a dog walker. While your friends are working 9-5, sitting in a cubicle or filing corporate reports, you are out enjoying the world around you, exploring new paths and walking familiar paths with a four-legged friend or two. It's really an amazing way to make a living. But it's not easy.

I hope this book has, in some way, been helpful to you. I am writing because I'm convinced that what I've learned

Afterword

in the last seven years of hands-on experience can help you succeed as a dog walker. I also am very aware that this book is simply a starting point. There are so many details, so many possible questions to answer, and every single situation is entirely unique.

If, after reading this book, you would want further help, I am available for consulting purposes. I really do want to help you succeed. And to be honest, I am still learning, as well. Leanne and I have built our dog walking business to the point where it is our primary source of income for our family of four, and we expect to continue to see our revenue and profits grow. I expect that we will continue to be in the dog walking business for years to come. It's a fun and exciting business, with new challenges all the time. Welcome to the wonderful world of dog walking. I hope you find incredible success!

For Consultation Information, go to www.vdogwalkers.com/business-consultation. I would love to give you a hand in further creating a sustainable dog walking business that can flourish and thrive, and provide you a livable income doing something you love.

I also wanted to include some of my documentation. I will include it here in the book, or you can download everything shown in the book at www.vdogwalkers.com/business-documentation. All our documents are free for you to take, copy, change, and use however you want.

Afterword

Consultation Paperwork – Seven Page Document Available for Download.

The first page is simply for collecting the potential client's basic information.

Client & Dog Information

Owner's Name:	Date:
Home Address:	
Home Phone:	Email:
Cell Phone:	
Work Phone:	
Dog Name / Breed / Age / Sex:	
Dog Name / Breed / Age / Sex:	
Dog Name / Breed / Age / Sex:	

Emergency Information

Emergency Contact:	Phone:
Vet Office / Vet's Name & Address:	Phone:
Current Medications:	Reason(s) for Meds:
Important Medical Notes:	

Ryan and Leanne Donovan – The Vancouver Dog Walkers
Phone: (360) 450-3647   Email: dogs@vdogwalkers.com   www.vdogwalkers.com

The second page is for clarifying the services they client is expecting to need, as well as making a plan for payment.

Description of Services and Payment Options

Type of Service
- Consistently Scheduled Service
- Needs Changing from Week to Week
- Sporadic / Occasional Service

Days of Walks for Consistently Scheduled Service:
- Monday
- Tuesday
- Wednesday
- Thursday
- Friday
- Saturday

Duration of Walks:
- 5 Min Potty Break
- 15 Min Walk
- 30 Min Walk
- 45 Min Walk
- 60 Min Walk

Window Of Time for Starting Walks:

Payment Options:
- Cash or Check
- Invoiced through PayPal
- Credit Card or Checking Account (EFT) on file
- Other:

Frequency of Payment:
- Pre-Pay (5 % Off for 10 pre-paid walks, 10% Off for 20 pre-paid walks)
- Pay at the End of Each Week
- Pay at the End of Every Two Weeks
- Pay at the End of the Month
- Other:

General Information

How Did You Hear About The Vancouver Dog Walkers?

Place to Put Poop Bags:

Dog's Known Behavior Issues (write on back of page if needed):

Ryan and Leanne Donovan – The Vancouver Dog Walkers
Phone: (360) 450-3647   Email: dogs@vdogwalkers.com   www.vdogwalkers.com

Afterword

The third page is our Liability Waiver and Policies. While we do everything to make sure the dogs we walk stay safe, it's important to be up front about the fact that there is always the possibility of a circumstance occurring that was beyond our ability to control.

Liability Waiver & Policies

Liability Waiver:
- I understand and accept sole responsibility for any harm to people, property, or other dogs caused by my dog(s) while my dog(s) are being cared for by The Vancouver Dog Walkers.
- I understand and agree that, in leaving my dog(s) under the supervision of The Vancouver Dog Walkers, I am acknowledging that my dog is currently in good health, and any known health concerns will be noted below.

    Known Health Concerns: _____

- I understand and agree that, besides gross negligence and/or willful misconduct, The Vancouver Dog Walkers will not be liable for any problems which develop or occur. Therefore, I hereby release The Vancouver Dog Walkers, as well as it's owners, employees and agents, from any liability which may arise during their care for my dog(s).
- I understand and agree that any health problems that develop with my dog will be treated as deemed best by The Vancouver Dog Walkers, in their sole discretion (after pursuing all possible owner / emergency contacts), and that I assume full financial responsibility for any and all expenses incurred.

Emergency Authorization:
I authorize emergency medical care to be provided by veterinarian I listed on this agreement, or an appropriate alternate to be determined by Ryan and Leanne Donovan and The Vancouver Dog Walkers, in the event that my regular veterinarian is not available or that closer care is required. I will reimburse Ryan and Leanne Donovan and The Vancouver Dog Walkers for any charges related to emergency care.

Holidays:
We are not available for dog walks on the following holidays: Easter, Mother's Day, Thanksgiving, Christmas Eve and Christmas Day.
We have a $5 holiday charge for the following days: Memorial Day, 4th of July, Labor Day

Cancellation Policy:
You are welcome to cancel any walks at any time. There will be no fee for any cancelled walks, except "at the door" cancellations, where we are not informed of the need to cancel until we arrive at your location. In the event of an "at the door" cancellation, we will charge our current rate for a 5 Minute Dog Potty Break. Currently that amount is $8, but is subject to change in the future.

Please Provide the Following:
- Adequate leashes and collars / harnesses for all dogs being walked.
- Towel we can use to dry dog, in the event dogs get wet during the walk.

I certify that I have read and understood this agreement. I agree to the terms and conditions stated in this agreement.

Name of Owner (Print): _____

Signature of Owner: _____ Date: _____

Ryan and Leanne Donovan – The Vancouver Dog Walkers
Phone: (360) 450-3647   Email: dogs@vdogwalkers.com   www.vdogwalkers.com

Suburban Dog Walking

The fourth page is a way to help assure our clients that we take their home security and privacy seriously, while also making sure we are on the same page about them giving us access to their house.

The Vancouver Dog Walkers Key and Home Entry Agreement

- In order to access my home, I will give The Vancouver Dog Walkers one or more of the following:

    Free Lockbox   Key   Home Entry Code   I Will Be Home   Other_____

- I understand that, in granting entry to my home for The Vancouver Dog Walkers, they will make enough copies of my key and/or share my home entry code or lockbox code, so that each of their employees who will visit and/or walk my dogs will be able to enter my home.

- I understand that The Vancouver Dog Walkers will, themselves, incur the cost of making duplicate keys for my home.

- I understand that the employees of The Vancouver Dog Walkers have agreed to keep my key safe, to never share or duplicate my key, or to enter my home except at the appropriate time for Dog Walking.

- I understand that, at any time, I am able to cancel my Dog Walking and ask to receive all copies of keys made for my home, as well as my original key.

I certify that I have read and understood this agreement. I agree to the terms and conditions stated in this agreement.

Sign: _____   Date: _____

Ryan and Leanne Donovan – The Vancouver Dog Walkers
Phone: (360) 450-3647   Email: dogs@vdogwalkers.com   www.vdogwalkers.com

Afterword

The fifth page explains our referral program, as well as the two standard discounts we offer. We offer a discount to people who are at least 65 years old, and we offer discounts to school teachers and administrators.

Current Discounts and Offers

VDW Referral Program

We love referrals! We love them so much, that we've decided to give a **permanent $1 per walk discount** for every person you refer who becomes a client. Here's how it works:

- **Step 1:** Tell a friend about our services.
- **Step 2:** Your friend starts using our services for a minimum of 5 separate visits.
- **Step 3:** You get a $1 discount on every walk we do with your dog forever.

Additionally, there is no end to the number of discounts you can receive from referrals. If you refer 5 people who end up using our services at least 5 times, you get a $5 discount per walk. So instead of a 30 minute dog walk for one dog costing $18, it would now only cost $13. Forever. The discount never goes away. Theoretically, you could refer so many people to us, that your walks become permanently free!

The Fine Print on the Referral Program

  *All Weekend and Evening Dog Walks, including discounted walks, still include a $5 charge. That $5 charge is not subject to the discount.

  **Discounted and Free Dog Walks limited to one per day, and only five days per week. A second walk in a day, or a sixth walk in a week, would be billed at the regular price.

  ***If you refer more people than the total needed for a free walk, the price for your walks is still free. We won't pay you when we come walk your dog. But if you're not careful, we might try to hire you to be our very first salesperson!

Standard Discounts

We recognize that life is expensive. We genuinely would love to be able to walk dogs for free! Although we can't do that, we have identified two groups of people who we are offering a special and unique discount on all walks. Those groups are **K-12 Teachers and Administrators** and **Seniors (65+)**. If you fit in one of those groups, let us know! The discount amounts are as follows:

- **$1 Per Walk Discount** for K-12 Teachers and Administrators
- **$1 Per Walk Discount** for Seniors (65+)

Ryan and Leanne Donovan – The Vancouver Dog Walkers
Phone: (360) 450-3647   Email: dogs@vdogwalkers.com   www.vdogwalkers.com

Suburban Dog Walking

The sixth page is a copy of the third page, as some clients like to keep a copy of what they signed.

Liability Waiver & Policies (Client Copy)

Liability Waiver:
- I understand and accept sole responsibility for any harm to people, property, or other dogs caused by my dog(s) while my dog(s) are being cared for by The Vancouver Dog Walkers.
- I understand and agree that, in leaving my dog(s) under the supervision of The Vancouver Dog Walkers, I am acknowledging that my dog is currently in good health, and any known health concerns will be noted below.

    Known Health Concerns: _____

- I understand and agree that, besides gross negligence and/or willful misconduct, The Vancouver Dog Walkers will not be liable for any problems which develop or occur. Therefore, I hereby release The Vancouver Dog Walkers, as well as it's owners, employees and agents, from any liability which may arise during their care for my dog(s).
- I understand and agree that any health problems that develop with my dog will be treated as deemed best by The Vancouver Dog Walkers, in their sole discretion (after pursuing all possible owner / emergency contacts), and that I assume full financial responsibility for any and all expenses incurred.

Emergency Authorization:
I authorize emergency medical care to be provided by veterinarian I listed on this agreement, or an appropriate alternate to be determined by Ryan and Leanne Donovan and The Vancouver Dog Walkers, in the event that my regular veterinarian is not available or that closer care is required. I will reimburse Ryan and Leanne Donovan and The Vancouver Dog Walkers for any charges related to emergency care.

Holidays:
We are not available for dog walks on the following holidays: Easter, Mother's Day, Thanksgiving, Christmas Eve and Christmas Day.
We have a $5 holiday charge for the following days: Memorial Day, 4th of July, Labor Day

Cancellation Policy:
You are welcome to cancel any walks at any time. There will be no fee for any cancelled walks, except "at the door" cancellations, where we are not informed of the need to cancel until we arrive at your location. In the event of an "at the door" cancellation, we will charge our current rate for a 5 Minute Dog Potty Break. Currently that amount is $8, but is subject to change in the future.

Please Provide the Following:
- Adequate leashes and collars / harnesses for all dogs being walked.
- Towel we can use to dry dog, in the event dogs get wet during the walk.

I certify that I have read and understood this agreement. I agree to the terms and conditions stated in this agreement.

Name of Owner (Print): _____

Signature of Owner: _____ Date: _____

Ryan and Leanne Donovan – The Vancouver Dog Walkers
Phone: (360) 450-3647   Email: dogs@vdogwalkers.com   www.vdogwalkers.com

Afterword

The seventh page is a copy of the fourth page, again, as some clients like to keep a copy of what they signed.

The Vancouver Dog Walkers Key and Home Entry Agreement (Client Copy)

- In order to access my home, I will give The Vancouver Dog Walkers one or more of the following:

  Free Lockbox   Key   Home Entry Code   I Will Be Home   Other_____

- I understand that, in granting entry to my home for The Vancouver Dog Walkers, they will make enough copies of my key and/or share my home entry code or lockbox code, so that each of their employees who will visit and/or walk my dogs will be able to enter my home.

- I understand that The Vancouver Dog Walkers will, themselves, incur the cost of making duplicate keys for my home.

- I understand that the employees of The Vancouver Dog Walkers have agreed to keep my key safe, to never share or duplicate my key, or to enter my home except at the appropriate time for Dog Walking.

- I understand that, at any time, I am able to cancel my Dog Walking and ask to receive all copies of keys made for my home, as well as my original key.

I certify that I have read and understood this agreement. I agree to the terms and conditions stated in this agreement.

Sign: _____   Date: _____

Ryan and Leanne Donovan – The Vancouver Dog Walkers
Phone: (360) 450-3647   Email: dogs@vdogwalkers.com   www.vdogwalkers.com

Check In Card – Available for Download as a Publisher File

We give each of our clients this check in card, and most stick it on the fridge with the magnet we provide. We sign and date the card each time we come for a walk, so they can see right away when they come home that there dog was walked each day.

THE VANCOUVER DOG WALKERS				
Min: 5 15 30 45 60 Date: Name: Eve Weekend Feed	Min: 5 15 30 45 60 Date: Name: Eve Weekend Feed	Min: 5 15 30 45 60 Date: Name: Eve Weekend Feed	Min: 5 15 30 45 60 Date: Name: Eve Weekend Feed	Min: 5 15 30 45 60 Date: Name: Eve Weekend Feed
Min: 5 15 30 45 60 Date: Name: Eve Weekend Feed	Min: 5 15 30 45 60 Date: Name: Eve Weekend Feed	Min: 5 15 30 45 60 Date: Name: Eve Weekend Feed	Min: 5 15 30 45 60 Date: Name: Eve Weekend Feed	Min: 5 15 30 45 60 Date: Name: Eve Weekend Feed
Min: 5 15 30 45 60 Date: Name: Eve Weekend Feed	Min: 5 15 30 45 60 Date: Name: Eve Weekend Feed	Min: 5 15 30 45 60 Date: Name: Eve Weekend Feed	Min: 5 15 30 45 60 Date: Name: Eve Weekend Feed	Min: 5 15 30 45 60 Date: Name: Eve Weekend Feed
Min: 5 15 30 45 60 Date: Name: Eve Weekend Feed	Min: 5 15 30 45 60 Date: Name: Eve Weekend Feed	Min: 5 15 30 45 60 Date: Name: Eve Weekend Feed	Min: 5 15 30 45 60 Date: Name: Eve Weekend Feed	Min: 5 15 30 45 60 Date: Name: Eve Weekend Feed

vdogwalkers.com | (360) 450-3647 | dogs@vdogwalkers.com

Afterword

Pricing Post Card – Available for download as a Publisher File. We bring this two-sided postcard to consultations, to make sure our clients are on the same page, regarding pricing. Also, we have them printed in color at a professional print shop, and they really look great, helping to give us a look of professionalism.

HONEST · DEPENDABLE · LOVE DOGS

vdogwalkers.com | (360) 450-3647 | dogs@vdogwalkers.com

WEEKDAY PRICING

5 Minute Backyard Potty Break
1, 2 or 3 Dogs $8

15 Minute Walk / Potty Break
1 Dog $14 - 2 Dogs $16

30 Minute Walk
1 Dog $18 - 2 Dogs $22

45 Minute Walk
1 Dog $22 - 2 Dogs $26

60 Minute Walk
1 Dog $26 - 2 Dogs $30

*Additional $5 charge for evening and weekend walks

Suburban Dog Walking

Bank Account / Credit Card Authorization Form –

Available for Download as a Word File.

We don't require our clients to keep a credit card on file, but we do provide that as one of our payment options.

Bank Account / Credit Card Payment Authorization Form

Schedule your payment to be automatically deducted from your bank account, or charged to your Visa, MasterCard, American Express or Discover Card. Just complete and sign this form to get started.

Here's How Recurring Payments Work:
You authorize regularly scheduled charges to your checking/savings account or credit card. You let us know the frequency that you would like to be charged, and we charge you the amount outstanding on your account at the frequency you choose. We will also send you an email invoice, detailing the charges we make.

Please complete the information below:

I, _____ (full name), authorize The Vancouver Dog Walkers to charge my bank account or credit card indicated below for the full amount of my outstanding balance for dog walks. I would like to be charged with the following frequency (circle one): **Monthly   Bi-weekly   Weekly**

Billing Address _____   Phone# _____
City, State, Zip _____   Email _____

Checking/ Savings Account   **Credit Card**
☐ Checking   ☐ Savings   ☐ Visa   ☐ MasterCard
Name on Acct _____   ☐ Amex   ☐ Discover
Bank Name _____   Cardholder Name _____
Account Number _____   Account Number _____
Bank Routing # _____   Exp. Date _____
Bank City/State _____

SIGNATURE _____   DATE _____

I understand that this authorization will remain in effect until I cancel it in writing, and I agree to notify The Vancouver Dog Walkers in writing of any changes in my account information or termination of this authorization. For ACH debits to my checking/savings account, I understand that because these are electronic transactions, these funds may be withdrawn from my account as soon as the above noted periodic transaction dates. In the case of an ACH Transaction being rejected for Non Sufficient Funds (NSF) I understand that The Vancouver Dog Walkers will contact me for payment. I also agree to reimburse The Vancouver Dog Walkers for any fees that may occur as a result of NSF. I acknowledge that the origination of ACH transactions to my account must comply with the provisions of U.S. law. I certify that I am an authorized user of this credit card/bank account and will not dispute these scheduled transactions with my bank or credit card company, so long as the transactions correspond to the terms indicated in this authorization form.

Additional Downloadable Items

Income and Expense Spreadsheet – A Jan-Dec Excel Spreadsheet for easily tracking the money that comes in and the money that goes out.

Walk and Payment Spreadsheet – A simple Excel Spreadsheet solution for tracking the walks for each dog, as well as for tracking payments received from each client.

Contact Ryan Donovan
dogs@vdogwalkers.com

ABOUT THE AUTHOR
Ryan Donovan

Ryan lives in Vancouver, WA with his wife, Leanne, and their daughters, Mabel and Estelle. In 2010, Ryan and Leanne started The Vancouver Dog Walkers out of a love for dogs and a desire to make a little money on the side. What started as a hobby business has now grown into a full-time career. Prior to, and in conjunction with operating The Vancouver Dog Walkers, Ryan spent 8 years as a pastor in a church. He left that role in the summer of 2016 to devote his full-time energy into running the dog walking business.

For more information, go to
www.vdogwalkers.com
or
www.vdogwalkers.com/suburbandogwalking